The Majesty The Mystery
And The Mission of Marriage

10/16/20

The Majesty The Mystery And The Mission of Marriage

John H. Dumke Sr.

Print information available on the last page.

Rev. date: 08/14/2020

To order additional copies of this book, contact:
Xlibris
844-714-8691
www.Xlibris.com
Orders@Xlibris.com
599615

Contents

Acknowledgements

Although there are indeed hundreds if not thousands of people who have influenced my life over these past 8 plus decades, I only have space to acknowledge a few who have been most instrumental in preparing me to write and to assure that this work would be published.

When I began this book, I was encouraged by a dear longtime friend, Kent Axtell of Phoenix Arizona, one of the most deeply spiritual people I know. Dick Bushnell gave me the book, "How to Live like a King's Kid" by Harold Hill. The message in that book put me on track to submit my will to Jesus Christ. Aaron Morris showed me what believing in the power of God and rejoicing in the midst of tribulations can do for a person who is really down and out. What a blessing and encouragement he has been to me. My parents Rev Allen and Mae Dumke always believed that God had something more for me to do than just take up space, as did my brothers Allen and David.

And when it came time to publish this work, these people made sure the resources were available, so a special thank you to Rev. Jeremy Grant, Mr. Bill Sapp, Mary Peters, and my sister Darlene and her husband, Rev. Robert L. Stuart, friends and family in the common faith once given to the saints.

The two most important influences in my life are first and foremost the Lord Jesus Christ, without whom we are all doomed, for we are redeemed by His blood and are hidden with Him in God awaiting that future day when we shall see Him in Glory and rejoice forevermore. I could have done nothing in this life without my Lord and Savior.

Only to God is Nita Raye second, for she is the one selected by Him to be my joy each day. She is my soul mate, my helper, my friend and wife, the completion of who I am, or as I like to say; "the rest of me."

Bio

John H. Dumke, Sr.

I was born April 22, 1940 to a farmer and his wife, Allen and Mae Dumke in Sanborn Minnesota. In 1943 Dad was called by the Spirit of God to leave the farm and to prepare for the Ministry. I was born again at age 7 in Hinton Iowa at my dad's first church. The next 31 years were spent in leaving home getting married, fathering 5 children, getting divorced, having my oldest son die at age 8, remarrying, adopting Nita's son and having another son with her, and questioning my earlier concepts and beliefs of God. I read "The Age of Reason" 1 & 2 by Thomas Paine, also a preacher's son, and I had pretty much left the Faith; BUT I just could not walk away, something kept nagging at me. One day a friend of mine, Dick Bushnell, gave me a book by Harold Hill, "How to live like a King's Kid", it lay on my bedside table for 3 weeks without being opened. Then one night I started reading and could not put it down. Somewhere around 2 A.M. I closed my eyes and prayed this prayer: "Lord I don't believe I have to ask you to come into my heart again because I did that as a child and I know you haven't left, but I see I have never submitted myself to you, I do that now." I closed my eyes and slept like I had not for weeks, then awoke a new man.

It took 30 years for me to submit and another 40 years to begin to understand and comply with His requests, however God is not in a hurry and as He spoke to me one time, He can do more in one year than I on my own can do in a lifetime.

Today I enjoy the life Nita Raye and I have together quietly, enjoying the autumn of our lives and with God in charge we can shine the brightest we ever have, because He will receive all the glory.

Walking with Jesus

John Henry Dumke Sr.

Introduction

It was the summer of 1996 and I was taking a walk meditating and praying about the future. I was fighting the feeling that I had wasted my life, that I had accomplished nothing of importance and that God was no doubt very disappointed in me and worst of all, most of my life was over.

What was I to say to Jesus when I saw Him? What excuse would suffice? None! It seemed I was destined to be just another man of promise who failed God and himself.

In the midst of this despair the Spirit of God spoke: "I want you to write a book on marriage." I wondered if this was just me thinking rather than God speaking, but I answered anyway.

I said, "There are so many more qualified people who could write it Lord, but if you want me to I'll do it." But, before I finished rejecting the idea, He said.

"I want you to title it;"

"The Majesty, The Mystery, and
The Mission of Marriage"

Now I knew the voice I heard was not from me but from Him and I was in awe. "Oh Father, how am I to do this and where do I start?"

"Start at the beginning." Is what I heard, so I began in Genesis and this book is what I discovered God has done to establish the institution of marriage and what He has instructed us to do in demonstrating to the world the reality of His great love.

I remember Kenneth Copeland said one time that God will give you a revelation and it can take 10 years to be able to tell it to the people. Although I have written a great deal about marriage and have spoken about what God has shown me, it has taken almost 10 years to come to the point of knowing the book must be written now. Today is New Year's Eve, 2005 and today the revelations God has given me are being put down on paper.

Much of what you will read may seem foreign to you because of tradition and culture, but please read everything with an open mind and spirit, then check it out scripturally and put into practice the concepts. I assure you your marriage will become what God intended it to be, a foretaste of Heaven, a joy beyond words.

Walking with Jesus
John H. Dumke

Ps. This book was originally written to be taught in a class in our Sunday School at Covenant Presbyterian Church in Omaha Nebraska. It is now being re-written to be a study book rather than a teaching manual, to make it a more enjoyable read and I think a more expansive discourse. However I believe you will gain more from it by reading and meditating on each chapter as if you were taking a 12 week course and that is particularly true as you begin to implement the practices God taught us as he guided us through the majesty and mystery and mission of the marriage covenant.

This book is a revised and updated version of the original published in 2013.

"The Majesty, The Mystery, and The Mission Of Marriage"

Division 1: The Majesty of Marriage

Week (1)   Introduction
             "Male and female created he them" to be a
             reflection of his love.
             Genesis 1:26- 28 & 2:21- 24: the royal act.

Week (2)   "Before I formed thee in the belly I knew
             thee"—
             a. The pre-existence of mankind: you and me?

             Jeremiah 1:5: pre-existence knowledge
             Ephesians 1:4-5: predestinated
             Revelation 13:8: Lamb slain from the
             foundation of the earth.

Week (3)   One becomes two in order for the two to
             become "One Flesh."

Genesis 1:26- 28: created as one;
Genesis 2:21- 24: separated to make two, brought together to be one.
Malachi 2:13-17: deal well with your wife.
1 Peter 3:7: Likewise, ye husbands, dwell with them
Matthew 19: 4-6: One flesh
Matthew 22:29-30: in heaven
John 17:20-23: that we may be one.
Ephesians 5:21-33: Submitting yourselves one to another

Week (4)   Creating as God creates. Only man has the god ability to create. Let's use what we were given to:
"Create a great mate."

Genesis 1 & 2: the creation process
John 1:1-5: all things were made by and for Christ.
Romans 4:17: calling those things that are not as though
they were.
Mark 11:12-14 & 22-24: Imagine, believe, speak, receive.

Division 2: The Mystery of Marriage

Week (5)   The parallel of Christ and the Church and man and wife, marriage.

Ephesians 5:28-33: The mystery of the parallel of Christ and the Church and man and wife, marriage.

Genesis 1:27 & 2:24: God saw them as a single entity

Genesis 3:22: God saw them sin as one entity.

Genesis 3:17: Blame fell on Adam

Genesis 3:17-19: Curse fell on both Adam and Eve as well as the earth.

Revelation 21:9: The Lord's bride.

Week (6)   How relations between a husband and wife parallel Christ and the Church.

Ephesians chapter 5: A godly marriage

John 17:23: I in them, and thou in me, that they may be made perfect,

Luke 15:4: "What man of you, having an hundred sheep, if he lose one,--

Matthew 11:28: "Come unto me all ye that labor and are heavy laden,

Acts: 16:31: "Believe on the Lord Jesus Christ and thou shalt be saved-."

Acts chapters 2-4: Detail the excitement of the new believers.

Galatians 2:1: Then 14 years after--."

Psalms 51:11-12: Cast me not away from thy presence;

John 17:23: I in them, and thou in me, that they may be made perfect,

Ephesians 4:13: "Till we all come in the unity of the faith,

Week (7)   How the husband is to be treated parallels how Christ is to be treated by the Church. How the wife is to be treated parallels how Christ treats the Church.

Galatians 3:28: In Gods eyes we are equals; Galatians 4:19: Christ is being formed in each of us.
Galatians 5:13-15;19--23 By love serving one another.
Colossians 3:12-14;18-19: Mercy, kindness and long Suffering.
I Corinthians 7:3-5: Power over our bodies belongs to the other.
Philippians 2:3&14: Esteem each other better.
Philippians 4:4-8: Rejoice.
Galatians 6:7; The law of sowing and reaping.
I Corinthians 13:1-8 Love.
I Corinthians 15:33: Evil communications.

Week (8)   Sexual relations in the Christian marriage.

Hebrews 13:4: Marriage bed is undefiled.
I Thessalonians 4:3-7: Possess your own vessel.

Song of Solomon: Sing a song of love to your spouse.
Proverbs 5:15-19: Be satisfied with your own spouse.
Proverbs 6:32: Adultery destroys.
I Corinthians 6:16: Adultery makes another "one" flesh!

Division III The Mission of Marriage.

Week (9)   What is the responsibility of the husband to his wife? What is the responsibility of the wife to her husband?

DUTIES OF A GODLY MAN
Genesis 3:23: Till the soil. (work to provide for his family.)
I Timothy 5:8: Man who does not provide has denied the faith.
Titus 2:6: Be sober minded.
Ephesians 5:25-33: Love wives as self.
Colossians 3:19: Love your wife and don't be bitter.
I Peter 3:7: Husband to give honor to his wife so their prayers are not hindered.

DUTIES OF A GODLY WIFE
Genesis 4:1: Only the wife is given the privilege of bringing new life into the world.
Proverbs 31:10-31: The model wife

Titus 2:4-5: She must be willing to learn and teach.

Colossians 3:18 & Ephesians 5:22-24: Wife is to submit to husband as the Church is to submit to Christ.

DUTIES OF BOTH HUSBAND AND WIFE

Genesis 1:28: Be fruitful, multiply, subdue the earth and have dominion.

Genesis 2:15: Dress the garden and keep it.

Ecclesiastes 4:9-10: Two, husband and wife, are better than one.

Ephesians 5:19-21: Give God thanks and submit to each other.

I Peter 5:5-9: Submit AND humble yourselves to each other.

Philippians 2:5-8: Have the mind of Christ, humble yet equal.

Colossians 3:12-14: Forgive one another and forbear one another.

Week (10) Our children are to be loved and trained in the same manner as God loves and trains us. We are to exhibit a God like character.

Proverbs 22: 6: Train up a child.

Proverbs 13:24 Spare the rod, spoil the child

Proverbs 3:11: Despise not the chastening of the Lord

Ephesians 6:4: rear in the fear and admonition of the Lord.

Colossians 3:21: Provoke not the children lest they become discouraged.

Week (11)   The marriage is to be a reflection of God's love to all God's creation but especially to mankind.
Ephesians 5:1-2: Be followers of Christ, reflect Him.
Galatians 4:19: Until Christ be formed in you.
John 17:21-23: That we may be one with Christ.

Week (12)   Mystery Revealed!! and challenge.
John 17:21-23: That we may be one with Christ.
Ephesians 5:28-33: The mystery of the parallel of Christ

FORWARD

No institution in all of history has come under as great an attack as Marriage, and for good reason. Marriage was established by God to be His example to His creation of His love for them. We humans have difficulty understanding concepts we cannot see illustrated. God knows that, after all He made us, so to show His love he invented Marriage. We, as Married people, are to love each other so deeply that our love becomes a visible expression of God's love for His creation. When we act this way, we bless our spouse as well as everyone who sees us. As a result of this we receive a many fold blessing as well from our Heavenly Father and creator.

For many years there has been a myriad of retreats, seminars, focus groups, sermons, books and lectures on Marriage and how to improve ours. Some of these are good, others not, but all in all well-intentioned people are doing what they can to help couples have a better Marriage and a more fulfilled life. It seems to me that most Marriage enrichment programs address the surface needs of the partners much like putting salve on a wound without seeking the origin of the problem, which is a proper understanding of <u>who</u> we are and <u>how</u> we are to conduct ourselves in a Christ-like way under the requirements of a God inspired covenant. We could call the old way of seminars an "I'm OK: you're OK" teaching. I believe programs like these can be helpful, but I would like to examine Marriage from God's point of view as explained in His word.

Why does Marriage matter? Why get Married? After all, in today's society it seems more than acceptable to have a relationship, be a significant other, live together, be together rather than make that life time commitment; "till death do us part." The first and most important answer is because this is what God our Father asks us to do. He has a reason, in fact a lot of reasons to have things done this way. We will be studying these reasons and the consequences of not following His plan throughout this teaching.

There are things in a Marriage that matter if we are to have a successful one. It is utterly startling, and amazing to me that we will spend countless days or weeks agonizing over a decision about the color of our new car, a new sofa, or drapes, but when it comes to deciding who we will spend a lifetime with we rely on the emotions of the moment more often than the directions of God.

Does God have a "Perfect Marriage plan"? The answer is; Yes!

OK, what is it? That is what we will answer from His word.

We, each of us, have responsibilities in our Marriages. You may say, "Well of course we do!" We have learned what these responsibilities are from our mothers, fathers, relatives, friends, and others. But can we say with certainty what God lists as our responsibilities? Unfortunately, most times, no.

Before we start, I would like you to join me in an introductory exercise.

Let us look at two absolutes.

(1) Jesus said when we accept Him as Lord and Savior, He and the Father would come and make their abode within us in the person of the Holy Spirit. Therefore, we can say with certainty that God lives within each of us and that includes our spouses.

(2) You have heard it said, "The eyes are the window to the soul." We know this from seeing the love of a mother when she looks at her child; a lover looking into the eyes of his beloved and the vacant stare of those who are lost in a world of insanity or evil.

Now, look into your spouse's eyes, I know this may be the first time you have consciously done this since before you were Married, but that's about to change!

Now think; you are looking into the face of God!! How could you treat this person with anything but love and devotion?

All right then, let us begin.

Chapter 1

The creation of mankind and marriage

The Royal Act

Scripture reading: Genesis 1:26- 28 & 2:21- 24:

Before we get into the discussion of marriage, we need a better understanding of who "man" is, how and why he was created and what was, and still is his purpose in this world? Why do we call this "The Royal Act", how does the creation of Man differ from all other creation? And why do we say Man and not man and woman?

I believe when we come to a real understanding of who we were created to be and what God has done to ensure our place in His Kingdom, our life will change for the better immediately. You are about to go from the valley of death and despair taught to you by the God deniers of the world, to the mountain top of exhilarated joy, unspeakable joy reserved for the children of Almighty God, Elohim!! I get excited and begin to shout His praises just thinking about this and I believe as we go through this revelation, you will start to shout too!

I teach a class at The Open Door Mission here in Omaha, Nebraska, called "Communications and Conflict Resolutions". I wrote the course and I teach it. Initially I was teaching a course someone else had written, and I told the Volunteer Director, that I could not use their material, because there was too much humanness and not enough God-ness. He let me write the teaching, and I did. It will be available online at amazon.com, if you want to teach it in your area of ministry.

Here is what I see in the people coming to my class. People created to look like God, recreated to be in Christ sitting on the seat next to God Almighty and having trouble wrapping their minds around who they are and what their rights and privileges are as children of the Most High God! They are coming out of despair, despondency, with the beginnings of a flicker of hope being crushed by the events of life, and the negative words coming from their own mouths as well as the mouths of the ones who should be helping them. They need a revelation of who they are, and I am the one God choose to tell them. Hallelujah!

My class is only one in a series of classes given daily over a 20 week period of time for people coming out of addictions. It is a fantastic program that not only graduates the students but continues to mentor them making sure they succeed in a world without the drugs or alcohol.

When I come into my classroom I go around to each person, shake their hand and speak a word of encouragement. When I see someone new, I introduce myself and tell them, "God loves you and He wants you in this class to learn about Him."

Then I tell the whole class, "You are children of the most high God! He loves you! You are special to Him! Your name is written on the palm of his hand! He loves you so much He sent His Son to die for you and now to live for you always interceding for you and speaking to you the words of life! Rejoice! Where you are right now is exactly where He wants you to be for your good and His glory. Don't fight it, embrace the God of the universe, jump up on His lap, throw your arms around His neck and kiss Him and say, "I love you Daddy!" Then squeeze His neck real tight and hang on because He is about to move the universe for His child, you!"

THAT DESCRIBES YOU AND YOUR SPOUSE TOO!

Why do I tell you all of this in a book about Marriage? Because you need to know who you are and who your spouse is before you will ever understand this beautiful thing called Marriage. You were created by God to be an under ruler, (under Him only), with dominion over all of creation! Did you know that? God the creator designed and built a home for His first couple, Adam, and Eve, before He created them. Later I will show you, He did the same thing for you; yes, he did!

This is what I want to tell you right now. God loves you and the Devil hates you! The Devil wants you to go to Hell and God is loving you into Heaven.

Here, then, is the real story of who you were created to be, and why Marriage is such an integral part of your creation.

But first I think we need to address an issue that began in Eden and has popped up its ugly head repeatedly throughout all of human history.

EVOLUTION

Evolution is nothing other than a denial of the existence of God the creator. Paul wrote in Romans 1:28-30

> Romans 1:28 And even as they did not like to retain God in *their* knowledge, God gave them over to a reprobate mind, to do those things which are not convenient;

> Romans 1:29 Being filled with all unrighteousness, fornication, wickedness, covetousness, maliciousness; full of envy, murder, debate, deceit, malignity; whisperers,

> Romans 1:30 Backbiters, haters of God, despiteful, proud, boasters, inventors of evil things, disobedient to parents,

It would do you well to read the entire first chapter of Romans, it is almost like reading the daily newspaper, so perfectly did Paul describe the attitude of the elitists of today.

Throughout all of history man has tried to replace God with himself and is still trying to do it today. From Eve in the Garden of Eden adding to the word of God, to Cain changing the type of sacrifice to bring to God, to the people of Noah's day, who had all abandoned the worship of God, to the ultimate sacrilege of the Tower of Babel, where the people not only chose to worship other gods, but added the sacrifice of humans created in the image and likeness of Almighty God, to their god, the god of this world or Satan, up and including the world in which we live, mankind continues to try to de-throne God.

I have news for them. Read Ezekiel chapter 28. Lucifer tried it and failed. Every world conqueror has tried to be God and has failed. And if you try it, you will fail. Enough said.

CREATION

The verses preceding man's creation, Genesis 1:1-20, detail the creation of the home for mankind, Eden. In all creation other than living beings from whales to mankind He imagined it, spoke it and it was so. The word used to create the world was "asah" which means to rearrange or make something out of material that already exists. The word used to describe the creation of living things including Mankind is "Bara", which means, "to bring into being" This is not reconstruction, it is something that had no pre-existence and is now created by God, an original!

MANKIND

In the following verses we see God creating "mankind", not just an individual. The use of the pronoun "them" helps us see the totality of His creation. I believe there is adequate proof in Scripture to see that when He created mankind, what I call AdamEve, He created JohnNita and you and your spouse. We will be investigating that further in the coming chapters.

Genesis 1:26

This is the beginning of the understanding of the Majesty of marriage, which starts with the majesty of man in the creation of the new species, the "likeness of God" species. Man is a spirit being and as such God created him to look just like Himself. You might say God cloned Himself to create mankind, then gave us an intelligence like His own so we could assist Him in co-creating, (mind and soul or nesesh), and finally gave each of us a slightly different looking suit, (body), to wear, perfectly suited for our environment. It would be a difficult world to live in if we all looked exactly alike, now wouldn't it?

Did God look in a heavenly mirror and simply create an exact spirit likeness? Did he create man to look like himself so that the rest of creation could see God the creator by looking at man? What did Satan see when he looked at the "likeness of God" man? He, like the rest of creation saw God! He hated man with a vicious hatred because man took his place as ruler of the earth and the "likeness of God" man looked just like God Himself! When man sinned, he obeyed Satan and in that obedience gave back to Satan the office of ruler of the earth. When Jesus paid the penalty for sin, or disobedience, He, Jesus, stripped the Devil of that authority and gave it to, not sinful mankind but rather to those people who accepted Him as Lord and Master and were OBEDIENT to Him. The title Christian is defined as "Christ like" or "likeness of Christ". Just as God the creator created mankind in His own image, Christ the savior creates the "born again" person in His image.

MALE AND FEMALE

Genesis 1:27

Did he create the new "likeness of God" to be male and female?

Let us consider the facts. What we often overlook is that God embodies all that is male and all that is female as is proven in Genesis 1:27.

> Genesis 1:27 So God created man in his *own* image, in the image of God created he him; male and female created he them.

Fact: He created mankind in His own image and in His own likeness then called that creation male and female before He took the female out of the original creation.

I will not try to list all the references that will substantiate that statement, but consider the times God nurtured his people, nursed his people and lovingly held his people in his embrace. These are actions and attributes most often associated with a mother or wife, or the female of our species.

If all the things listed in Genesis 1:1-25 were done in preparation of the introduction of His image being placed in this environment, we must ask the question, for what purpose?

<u>Be fruitful, multiply and replenish the earth.</u>

> Genesis 1:28 And God blessed them, and God said unto them, Be fruitful, and multiply, and replenish the earth, and subdue it: and have dominion over the fish of the sea, and over the fowl of the air, and over every living thing that moveth upon the earth.

The new "likeness of God" species were to have children and fill the earth with "likenesses of God! The purpose was to bring glory to God in all of creation. Everywhere the creatures looked they would see "God". Every person would see God in every other person because everyone looked like God and reminded all who saw them of God and His goodness.

When people see Christians today what they should see is the "likeness of Christ". I am speaking from a spiritual standpoint. Spirits see their own kind. I have seen the Spirit of God residing in a person, recognize and respond to the Spirit of God residing in another person even though the people didn't know each other.

Have dominion over all of creation

In this we see the God like qualities given to us as members of the "likeness of God" species. Adam had and lost through disobedience, total authority over all of God's creation.

Adam was the god of this world, what he said was as it would be. At that point in time we could say, just as the Word says about God saying, "Adam said and it was so!" He could and did act just like God! Wow! Did you ever think about what great power and authority was Adam's from the beginning of creation? I have a point to this thought. As Christians we have been given dominion over the Devil and his forces. We simply must learn to exercise that authority by acting out who we are, having been recreated in the "likeness of Christ." We can not afford to give our authority to God's enemy as Adam did, by non-use or misuse of our rights.

THE ABILITY TO CREATE

Then God did something special for only mankind. He gave us His own "God" ability to imagine, or to see "the end from the beginning". Architects SEE the building before one brick is laid. Writers of music HEAR the song before writing it down; painters SEE the finished picture before the first brush stroke. This cannot be done by any other of God's creation.

God gave mankind the ability to take that picture in our minds and using the laws He established, create, or build what we "see". No other of God's creation has built a home, hospital, or a road, or any of the everyday activities we simply do.

A HOME FOR MANKIND

> Genesis 2:15 And the LORD God took the man, and put him into the garden of Eden to dress it and to keep it.

We have a picture in our minds of Eden being a place where one could lay in a hammock and sip iced tea. Not so! God gave Adam and Eve duties to keep them busy. You see, only man has the "God" ability to co-create with Him, but also the responsibility to accomplish tasks. Their first duty was to have children. Their second was subdue the earth, to work the soil to cause the plants to thrive and produce to their capacity. Then we see the "foreman", God the creator, stopping by in the "cool of the day", Genesis 3:8, to receive a report of the day's activity. Man was made to work. Look at any of the animals, birds, or fish, they spend most of their time foraging for food and sleeping. God gave man all he needed for food so he, man, could spend his time accomplishing creative goals. And God gave man dominion over all living creation. Wow!

Jesus promised us that if we would, "seek first the kingdom of God and His righteousness", (Matthew 6:33), all the other things would be given to us without the daily struggle of foraging or in our case fighting each other for the necessities of life. Actually, this blessing began in Eden.

> Genesis 1:29 And God said, Behold, I have given you every herb bearing seed, which *is* upon the face of all the earth, and every tree, in the which *is* the fruit of a tree yielding seed: to you it shall be for meat.

> Matthew 6:33 But seek ye first the kingdom of God, and his righteousness: and all these things shall be added unto you.

DRESS IT, KEEP OR PROTECT IT

> Genesis 2:15 And the LORD God took the man and put him into the garden of Eden to dress it and to keep it.

This was the great sin, or missing the mark or target, of Adam and Eve. They were instructed to protect the garden, but from whom? They were instructed to protect the garden from anyone or anything that would come against it. Really, they had all they needed to defeat any intruder.

They had the words of God, the directive from God and the name of God. (Surprise we have the same tools!)

That awful afternoon at the tree of the knowledge of good and evil could have been and should have been the final defeat of God's enemy, Satan. All Adam and Eve had to do to protect the garden and themselves was to speak the words of God, (look at what the Centurion said to Jesus; "but speak the word only." Matthew 8:8), They had the authority to command the Satan controlled serpent to depart. They had dominion! God gave it to them! They had the tools to defeat their enemy and they did not use them. Instead they doubted God and His word and agreed with the enemy and it cost them their lives and the fall of all mankind. They gave up their inheritance over ALL of God's creation and that included Satan, because of pride.

They wanted to be as God, to know the difference between good and evil.

> Genesis 3:4 And the serpent said unto the woman, Ye shall not surely die: Genesis 3:5 For God doth know that in the day ye eat thereof, then your eyes shall be opened, and ye shall be as gods, knowing good and evil.

Notice what Satan did. First, he called God a liar in verse 4 by stating that though they would be disobeying Him by eating from the tree of knowledge, they would not surely die. Then in verse 5 he said in effect "You think God is so good to you and all the time he is holding back knowledge, the knowledge that will allow you to be just like him, a god, knowing good and evil." The Devil never changes. His tactics have remained the same since the beginning of time. After all, why change if what he does is so successful? Pride is the spirit that corrupted Lucifer the anointed Cherub and Mankind's relationship with God.

> Ezekiel 28:14 Thou *art* the anointed cherub that covereth; and I have set thee *so:* thou wast upon the holy mountain of God; thou hast walked up and down in the midst of the stones of fire.

> Ezekiel 28:15 Thou *wast* perfect in thy ways from the day that thou wast created, till iniquity was found in thee.

Pride made him Satan and the Devil, and now he uses what was used on him, pride, to steal, kill, and destroy mankind. Just as Adam and Eve had a choice, obey or disobey God, so do we and the spirit of pride is always close by to try to deceive us, to convince us that we can and should "do it our own way, to be the captain of our own ship, to be in control of our own lives," or in other words to be our own god! It never works and we always fail when we try to replace God, when we try to sit on His throne.

THE FIRST MARRIAGE

Genesis 2:22 And the rib, which the LORD God had taken from man, made he a woman, and brought her unto the man.

Genesis 2:23 And Adam said, This *is* now bone of my bones, and flesh of my flesh: she shall be called Woman, because she was taken out of Man.

Genesis 2:24 Therefore shall a man leave his father and his mother, and shall cleave unto his wife: and they shall be one flesh.

This is the history of the first wedding performed by God himself!

In Genesis 1:26&27 God created mankind, male and female, he now separates the female from the male to make two where one existed before, so that he could bring them together in a marriage covenant that sees them to be "one flesh". This is to be a reflection of the oneness of a triune God, one God in three persons. So, who is the third person of the marriage covenant? God!

Look at Jesus' beautiful prayer in John 17:20-23.

John 17:20 Neither pray I for these alone, but for them also which shall believe on me through their word;

John 17:21 That they all may be one; as thou, Father, *art* in me, and I in thee, that they also may be one in us: that the world may believe that thou hast sent me.

John17:22 And the glory which thou gavest me I have given them; that they may be one, even as we are one:

John 17:23 I in them, and thou in me, that they may be made perfect in one; and that the world may know that thou hast sent me, and hast loved them, as thou hast loved me.

Here we see the perfect union, God + husband + wife = the Majesty of Marriage.

There is majesty about man that can only come from God, it is His exclusively, and that makes us reflections of Him to His other creation. In the marriage covenant God carries this forward to show that the love and devotion exhibited in that relationship is to be a reflection of the great love He has for mankind. When we demean, degrade, curse or in any way abuse our mate, we dishonor God.

Let's review what God did in the creation of mankind.

(1) Man was made in the very image and likeness of God.
(2) God gave Man dominion over all His creation.
(3) Adam was given the mind of God which allows him to imagine things that cannot be seen and create them.
(4) He gave man the right and ability to co-create with Him using the same tools, words, belief or faith, and expectancy.

TWO FINAL TRUTHS

There are two more things I want you to see before we close this chapter. Number one, what you and I have been given, first by being created by God and then redeemed by the blood of Christ at Calvary; we have our rights and authority restored! Hallelujah! It is time we start taking God at His word. If God said it, that settles it, so be it! Amen.

Look what Jesus said in Mark 11:22-26

> Mark 11:22 And Jesus answering saith unto them, Have faith in God.
>
> Mark 11:23 For verily I say unto you, That whosoever shall say unto this mountain, Be thou removed, and be thou cast into the sea; and shall not doubt in his heart, but shall believe that those things which he saith shall come to pass; he shall have whatsoever he saith.
>
> Mark 11:24 Therefore I say unto you, What things soever ye desire, when ye pray, believe that ye receive *them,* and ye shall have *them.*
>
> Mark 11:25 And when ye stand praying, forgive, if ye have ought against any: that your Father also which is in heaven may forgive you your trespasses.
>
> Mark 11:26 But if ye do not forgive, neither will your Father which is in heaven forgive your trespasses.

That brings us to number two, the words we speak. In James chapter 3 we are told that a mature Christian will not offend in "word", that he controls his tongue.

> James 3:2 For in many things we offend all. If any man offend not in word, the same *is* a perfect man, *and* able also to bridle the whole body.

It will greatly enlighten you in the power of words if you will read the first 12 verses of chapter three.

God created man with words, then gave man the ability to do the same thing He does, create with words. The enemy has convinced us to use this creative tool to destroy, especially in the marriage relationship.

Although the truths here are applicable to all Christians they are even more to the Christian husband and wife.

As we bring this lesson to a close let us look at God's idea of "one".

> Genesis 2:18 "And the Lord God said; It is not good that the man should be alone; I will make him an help meet for him."

> A synonym for alone is, one. So let us read it that way.

*And the Lord God said, "It is not good that the man should be **one**; I will make him an help meet for him."*

> *In Ecclesiastes 4:9-12 we find that truth in common everyday experiences. Let's read them.*

Ecclesiastes 4:9 Two *are* better than one; because they have a good reward for their labour.

Ecclesiastes 4:10 For if they fall, the one will lift up his fellow: but woe to him *that is* alone when he falleth; for *he hath* not another to help him up.

Ecclesiastes 4:11 Again, if two lie together, then they have heat: but how can one be warm *alone?*

Ecclesiastes 4:12 And if one prevail against him, two shall withstand him; and a threefold cord is not quickly broken.

And now let's read the mystery of this in Ephesians 5:25-29

Ephesians 5:25 Husbands, love your wives, even as Christ also loved the church, and gave himself for it;

Ephesians 5:26 That he might sanctify and cleanse it with the washing of water by the word,

Ephesians 5:27 That he might present it to himself a glorious church, not having spot, or wrinkle, or any such thing; but that it should be holy and without blemish.

Ephesians 5:28 So ought men to love their wives as their own bodies. He that loveth his wife loveth himself.

Ephesians 5:29 For no man ever yet hated his own flesh; but nourisheth and cherisheth it, even as the Lord the church:

Men, you can show no greater love for yourself than to love your wife, unconditionally. You are no longer an "I" you are we and us.

Some time ago a good Christian friend was making a confession of a fault for the use of his time and resources to a few of us who he knew would be understanding and would pray for and with him. When he finished talking, without thinking about what I would say these words flew out of my mouth: "As soon as I am perfect, I will criticize you."

That is good advice for all of us in all relationships, but especially in the marriage relationship. Keep following this rule and you will change as will your spouse. We do need to counsel and advise people when asked to, or when led to by the Spirit of God, but not to criticize.

The Jesus parallel is obvious in this lesson, as Jesus gave Himself for us, for our benefit, with less regard for Himself than for us, so we are to give ourselves to each other with the same abandonment.

Our "Action for Creation" for this week is:

I will not criticize; I will compliment only.

LOVE NOTES FROM JOHN
TO HIS LOVE

EVERY MORNING
IS A GLORIOUS MORNING
BECAUSE OF YOU.

Chapter 2

The creation of you

Our "Action for Creation" for this week was:

I will not criticize; I will compliment only.

So how are you doing? What changes are you beginning to see in each other, especially in yourselves? Scripture readings for this week are:

> Jeremiah 1:5 "Before I formed thee in the belly I knew thee"—
> Ephesians 1:4-5 According as He hath chosen us--
> Revelation 13:8 –the Lamb slain from the foundation--

The pre-existence of mankind: you and me?
I was not sure if I should teach on this subject because in our culture it stretches to the edge of our imagination. However as for me, I believe we did exist before we arrived on earth if in no other way then in the heart and mind of God. And I believe we have

adequately proven that from the Scriptures we just read.

What settled the issue with me as to whether or not teach on this, was a conversation I had with a longtime friend and Christian confidant. We were discussing the marriage study when I mentioned this section and the belief I have. Our conversation went something like this:

"Are you aware the Hebrew language has a word for the person you are to marry as if this arrangement was made in heaven before the birth of the man or the woman? You see, in Hebrew antiquity the BERSHIT, (male), has a BERSHERAH, (female) who is his soul mate, and he is to find her, join her in marriage to fulfill their destiny. The belief in antiquity was that if you married someone else the marriage would fail!"

His response was a stunned gasp! You see, he and his first wife divorced while both were Christians!

I said, "Did God take a burden off you with that truth?"

He said: "We have to talk about this soon. I want to know what has been revealed to you."

So let's talk.

Let's go back to the Old Testament.

> Jeremiah 1:5 Before I formed thee in the belly I knew thee; and before thou camest forth out of the womb I sanctified thee, and I ordained thee a prophet unto the nations.

"Before I formed thee in the belly, I knew thee-!" Think about that for a minute. God is no respecter of persons, so he knew you and me before He formed us! Wow! And how?

This Scripture begs several questions.

(1) If God knew Jeremiah before he was formed, in what context did He know him?

(2) Where were they, Jeremiah and God, when He knew him?

(3) Did they know each other in a heavenly pre-existence? Or did God know Jeremiah, but Jeremiah was not aware of it?

The correct way to read and understand Scripture is to take it literally unless there is a definite other understanding. Here, we see God calling Jeremiah into service for Himself and, He needed to make Jeremiah understand that this call was from the one who had known him and had called him from the beginning of time and had called him for a purpose which He, God, would lead him through, and to "prove" it, as it were, He, God, said, "I knew you before I formed you."

Isn't it amazing how many times God has to do the same thing to you and to me?

I want you to think about your life. There have been times when you "knew" what you were to do, as if a voice was directing you, and you didn't do it because you couldn't figure out the how, where, when of it. That is exactly where Jeremiah found himself. But what he did was trust God. And when you read through the book that bears his name, you will find some really strange things God had him do. I am sure friends and family thought he was crazy most of the time, and when you answer the call of God, some of your closest friends will think the same of you.

As I am rewriting this book, changing it from a teaching manual to a personal study book, I have started a new work titled; "I am a Simple Man with a Simple Faith: Who added all the Junk?." In it I ask the question; "If Christianity is such a simple God to man relationship teaching, so simple in fact that most of the known world accepted it within the first century, who added all the junk?" We lose the power of God when we add traditions or as I call them, junk, to the simple word of God.

> *Mark 7:13 Making the word of God of none effect through your tradition, which ye have delivered: and many such like things do ye.*

Let us look at other pre-existing passage from the New Testament.

> Ephesians 1:4 According as he hath chosen us in him before the foundation of the world, that we should be holy and without blame before him in love:

We see in this Scripture that God "hath chosen us before the foundation of the world" and that he "predestinated us unto the adoption of children by Jesus Christ".

The fact that we were chosen and predestinated before the foundation of the world tells us that from God's view point we were in existence:

(1) before the foundation of the world was laid, therefore.
(2) before the world was created, therefore:
(3) before Adam and Eve were created, therefore,
(4) before any of our ancestors lived, therefore.
(5) before my parents were born, therefore.
(6) before I was born, therefore.
(7) before I was conceived!

You were chosen by God to spend eternity with Him, but He also gave you free choice. You have the right to say "no"!

The Scripture that settled this issue of pre-existence for me is in the revelation given to the Apostle John on the Isle of Patmos.

> Revelation 13:8 And all that dwell upon the earth shall worship him, whose names are not written in the book of life of the Lamb slain from the foundation of the world.

"- the Lamb slain from the foundation of the world."

There would be no reason for the "Lamb" to be slain were it not for the existence of you and me.

Obviously, this concept brings a whole new series of questions, but let us look at the simplicity of it.

(1) Did we exist in some form in the presence of God from the foundation of the world?
(2) Were we created at the same time Adam, male and female, were created?
(3) Was our presentation to the earth simply delayed fulfilling God's purposes for us?
(4) Were we created with our own Adam or Eve and will our lives be unfulfilled without that connection?

To me the answer to all these questions is, yes! God created us, and knew us and loved us and planned for our arrival on earth and prepared a home for us, a life for us and made all the "plan B's" when we didn't follow His plan.

How detailed is God's plan for your life? As His child every minute of every day has His purpose and blessing.

I want to tell you three stories about this wonderful Father we have and how He works in people's lives to bring His plans to fruition. One story you don't know yet, but the other two you have read and will remember.

King David, a man after God's own heart, had an affair with Bathsheba, the wife of one of his own military leader's and when she became pregnant,

David had her husband killed, then married her and they had a son.

God sent His prophet to King David and exposed his sin, David repented, saw his ill-gotten son die, then had another son with Bathsheba, named Solomon, and this son became king after David.

Wait there is something else! Solomon is in the linage of Jesus, God's only begotten son! God took the mess of this situation and brought about the world's Messiah! Believe me, there is nothing you have done or could do that is beyond God's ability to correct and eventually make your mistake into a blessing. God will take the garbage of your life and turn it into the best soil in His garden if you will let Him.

Our second case is that of a girl who marries, had no children and was widowed just 7 years later. She took up residence in the Temple and spent her time serving God with fasting and prayers and was still there when she turned 84 years old. What all did she do? From a human standpoint it looks like a dull and sorrowful life, until Joseph and Mary brought Jesus in to "do all things according to the law of the Lord" and seeing Jesus. Anna sang a song of praise to Almighty God which you and I read every Christmas season! (Luke 2:36-38)

This last case is personal. Both my wife Nita Raye and I Had been married before we met, and both of us knew almost from the start that our spouses were not the ones we were to supposed to marry, they were not our soul mates.

When we met, we were both divorced, she had 1 child, and I had 5. We met the day after Thanksgiving 1965. By December 15th, I told her I thought we could get married and never regret it. On April 14th, 1966 we were married and now all these years later, we are more in love than ever.

I always felt that in the first marriage there were two gears trying to mesh but always missed. When I got to know Nita Raye, the gears meshed perfectly because I was created with her as one flesh, before the foundation of the world! She is my BERSHERAH!

Now for an especially important thought. You are to accept that the person you are with today is your soul mate. Do not go looking elsewhere.

The Jesus parallel in this lesson is, as Christ gave Himself for us from the foundation of the world, so should we give ourselves to our spouses unconditionally and for eternity.

Our "Action for Creation" for this week is:

Speak only building up words to and about your spouse.

LOVE NOTES FROM JOHN
TO HIS LOVE

I WOKE IN THE NIGHT
LOOKED AT YOU
AND WHISPERED A PRAYER
OF THANKSGIVING FOR THE
BLESSING OF YOUR LOVE.

Chapter 3

One Flesh

Our "Action for Creation" for this week was:

Speak only building up words to
and about your spouse.

So how are you doing? What changes are you beginning to see in each other, especially in yourselves? Our Scripture readings for this week are:

Genesis 1:26- 28: created as one;
Genesis 2:21- 24 separated to make two, brought together to be one flesh.
Malachi 2:13-17: deal well with your wife.
1 Peter 3:7 Likewise, ye husbands, dwell with them
Matthew 19: 4-6: One flesh
Matthew 22:29-30: in heaven
John 17:20-23: that we may be one.
Ephesians 5:21-33: Submitting yourselves one to another

Have you noticed that we always start with Genesis? The reason, of course is, everything begins in Genesis. Genesis is the foundation of our Faith and Belief system. If Genesis is not true, then nothing is true.

Here is the progression of God's plan for His man in creation.

Genesis 1:26 And God said, Let us make man in our image, after our likeness:

(1) God creates a human race in one unit. He calls the unit man.

(2) Man is made in the image and likeness of the Creator.

(3) Every attribute of male and female is in God, therefore they must be so in the new creation, mankind.

(4) It was God's decision to have Man be separated into two units to fulfill His purposes.

(5) He then took the two people, one male and one female and brought them together in a Blood Covenant.

(6) A Blood Covenant cannot be broken except by the death of one of the partners to the covenant.

(7) God has used the Blood Covenant of marriage to illustrate His own Covenant with us which He sealed in His own blood.

In Malachi we see the seriousness with which God holds the marriage covenant. The Israelites were wearing God out with the way the men were treating there wives.

> Malachi 2:13 And this have ye done again, covering the altar of the LORD with tears, with weeping, and with crying out, insomuch that he regardeth not the offering any more, or receiveth *it* with good will at your hand.

> Malachi 2:14 Yet ye say, Wherefore? Because the LORD hath been witness between thee and the wife of thy youth, against whom thou hast dealt treacherously: yet *is* she thy companion, and the wife of thy covenant.

> Malachi 2:15 And did not he make one? Yet had he the residue of the spirit. And wherefore one? That he might seek a godly seed. Therefore take heed to your spirit, and let none deal treacherously against the wife of his youth.

> Malachi 2:16 For the LORD, the God of Israel, saith that he hateth putting away: for *one* covereth violence with his garment, saith the LORD of hosts: therefore take heed to your spirit, that ye deal not treacherously.

> Malachi 2:17 Ye have wearied the LORD with your words. Yet ye say, Wherein have we wearied *him?* When ye say, Every one that doeth evil *is* good in the sight of the LORD, and he delighteth in them; or, Where *is* the God of judgment?

Peter writes in 1 Peter 3:7 that our prayers will not be answered when we ignore our marriage covenant.

> 1 Peter 3:7 Likewise, ye husbands, dwell with *them* according to knowledge, giving honor unto the wife, as unto the weaker vessel, and as being heirs together of the grace of life; that your prayers be not hindered.

In Matthew 19: 4-6 we see Jesus state the concept of Genesis, thereby establishing it as a commandment for us today.

> Matthew 19:4 And he answered and said unto them, Have ye not read, that he which made them at the beginning made them Male and female,

> Matthew 19:5 And said, For this cause shall a man leave father and mother, and shall cleave to his wife: and they twain shall be one flesh?

> Matthew 19:6 Wherefore they are no more twain, but one flesh. What therefore God hath joined together, let not man put asunder.

In Matthew 22 Jesus answered the Sadducees explaining the reality of heaven. This does not mean we will be sexless; it means that there is no need to have offspring. I will be a male and Nita will be a female, but it also appears we will be as we were before our entrance into this world, one. Just as God the Father is one entity, as is Jesus and the Holy Spirit, yet one God. In this world a married couple is one flesh. In the next world we will be one soul and one spirit yet individual.

Matthew 22:29 Jesus answered and said unto them, Ye do err, not knowing the scriptures, nor the power of God.

Matthew 22:30 For in the resurrection they neither marry, nor are given in marriage, but are as the angels of God in heaven.

The prayer of Jesus in John the 17 chapter is one of the most important Scriptures in the Bible, if not the most important. Here Jesus prays to the Father stating what He wants life for the believer to be. Let's read it and look at the requests together.

John 17:1 These words spake Jesus, and lifted up his eyes to heaven, and said, Father, the hour is come; glorify thy Son, that thy Son also may glorify thee:

John 17:2 As thou hast given him power over all flesh, that he should give eternal life to as many as thou hast given him.

John 17:3 And this is life eternal, that they might know thee the only true God, and Jesus Christ, whom thou hast sent.

John 17:4 I have glorified thee on the earth: I have finished the work which thou gavest me to do.

John 17:5 And now, O Father, glorify thou me with Thine own self with the glory which I had with thee before the world was.

John 17:6 I have manifested thy name unto the men which thou gavest me out of the world: Thine they were, and thou gavest them me; and they have kept thy word.

John 17:7 Now they have known that all things whatsoever thou hast given me are of thee.

John 17:8 For I have given unto them the words which thou gavest me; and they have received *them,* and have known surely that I came out from thee, and they have believed that thou didst send me.

John 17:9 I pray for them: I pray not for the world, but for them which thou hast given me; for they are Thine.

John 17:10 And all mine are Thine, and Thine are mine; and I am glorified in them.

John 17:11 And now I am no more in the world, but these are in the world, and I come to

John 17:12 While I was with them in the world, I kept them in thy name: those that thou gavest me I have kept, and none of them is lost, but the son of perdition; that the scripture might be fulfilled.

John 17:13 And now come I to thee; and these things I speak in the world, that they might have my joy fulfilled in themselves.

John 17:14 I have given them thy word; and the world hath hated them, because they are not of the world, even as I am not of the world.

John 17:15 I pray not that thou shouldest take them out of the world, but that thou shouldest keep them from the evil.

John 17:16 They are not of the world, even as I am not of the world.

John 17:17 Sanctify them through thy truth: thy word is truth.

John 17:18 As thou hast sent me into the world, even so have I also sent them into the world.

John 17:19 And for their sakes I sanctify myself, that they also might be sanctified through the truth.

John 17:20 Neither pray I for these alone, but for them also which shall believe on me through their word;

John 17:21 That they all may be one; as thou, Father, *art* in me, and I in thee, that they also may be one in us: that the world may believe that thou hast sent me.

John 17:22 And the glory which thou gavest me I have given them; that they may be one, even as we are one:

John 17:23 I in them, and thou in me, that they may be made perfect in one; and that

the world may know that thou hast sent me, and hast loved them, as thou hast loved me.

John 17:24 Father, I will that they also, whom thou hast given me, be with me where I am; that they may behold my glory, which thou hast given me: for thou lovedst me before the foundation of the world.

John 17:25 O righteous Father, the world hath not known thee: but I have known thee, and these have known that thou hast sent me.

John 17:26 And I have declared unto them thy name, and will declare *it:* that the love wherewith thou hast loved me may be in them, and I in them.

If ever a prayer has been, or will be answered, this one will. This is a prayer from an obedient Son to His Heavenly Father. The Father heard this prayer and is making sure every request is fulfilled! We know from the Scriptures we have read, that God answers the prayers of obedient children. If your prayers are not being answered, the hold up in on our part, not on God's. Sometimes we can't figure out what is wrong, if that is the case follow God's direction in the letter James wrote to believers;

James 1:5 If any of you lack wisdom, let him ask of God, that giveth to all *men* liberally, and upbraideth not; and it shall be given him.

Let us now go to Ephesians 5:21-33

Ephesians 5:21 Submitting yourselves one to another in the fear of God.

Ephesians 5:22 Wives, submit yourselves unto your own husbands, as unto the Lord.

Ephesians 5:23 For the husband is the head of the wife, even as Christ is the head of the church: and he is the saviour of the body.

Ephesians 5:24 Therefore as the church is subject unto Christ, so *let* the wives *be* to their own husbands in every thing.

Ephesians 5:25 Husbands, love your wives, even as Christ also loved the church, and gave himself for it;

Ephesians 5:26 That he might sanctify and cleanse it with the washing of water by the word,

Ephesians 5:27 That he might present it to himself a glorious church, not having spot, or wrinkle, or any such thing; but that it should be holy and without blemish.

Ephesians 5:28 So ought men to love their wives as their own bodies. He that loveth his wife loveth himself.

Ephesians 5:29 For no man ever yet hated his own flesh; but nourisheth and cherisheth it, even as the Lord the church:

Ephesians 5:30 For we are members of his body, of his flesh, and of his bones.

Ephesians 5:31 For this cause shall a man leave his father and mother, and shall be joined unto his wife, and they two shall be one flesh.

Ephesians 5:32 This is a great mystery: but I speak concerning Christ and the church.

Ephesians 5:33 Nevertheless let every one of you in particular so love his wife even as himself; and the wife *see* that she reverence *her* husband.

Here are the points we want to see:

(1) In verse 21 we see a Christian principal that makes for a Christ-like life. And it means what it says. Husbands are to submit to their wives in faith. And wives are to submit to their husbands in faith. There are religions and denominations whose theology puts the women in a second-class status, and men as rulers over them. That is wrong, period. It demeans God, for we, male and female are created in His image. To demean women is to demean God! Sounds like Satan's lie to Adam and Eve in Genesis 3:4-5.

(2) Verse 25 states that husbands are to lay down their lives for their wives. That means we men are to cast aside all bachelorhood things and devote ourselves to our wives. It does not mean that wives should order their husband around as we have all seen some do, but rather when a wife reverences her husband as the Church does Christ, the response from her husband

will be to offer his life to her as Christ has done for the Church.

(3) Men are to love their wives as their own bodies. When he loves his wife, he is loving himself! How can this be? except they be one.

(4) This is repeated in verse 33 to add emphasis and instruction for the wife to reverence her husband.

The Jesus parallel in this lesson is, as Jesus prayed that we as Christians should be one, we as a married couple should be even more committed to oneness.

Our "Action for Creation" for this week is:

It is no longer I who live but we, for we are one.

LOVE NOTES FROM JOHN
TO HIS LOVE

IF GOD HAD NOT CREATED
YOU FOR ME TO LOVE,
I WOULD HAVE HAD
TO IMAGINE YOU.
FOR ME THERE CAN BE
NOTHING BUT EMPTINESS
WITHOUT YOU

Chapter 4

Create a great mate

Our "Action for Creation" for this week was:

It is no longer I who live but we, for we are one.

So how are you doing? What changes are you beginning to see in each other, especially in yourselves?

Creating as God creates. Only man has the God ability to create. Let's use what we were given to: "Create a great mate."

Scripture readings for this week are:

> Genesis 24: Rebekah is found for Isaac
> John 1:1-5: all things were made by and for Christ.
> Romans 4:17: calling those things that are not as though they were.
> Mark 11:12-14 & 22-24: imagine, believe, speak, receive

We all have heard the beautiful story found in Genesis Chapter 24, of Isaac and Rebekah, how Abraham sent his servant to his, Abrahams, people to bring a wife for his son and how the servant spoke words for God to use to bring the chosen one for Isaac to him. God honored that prayer and the words spoken, and the chosen wife for Isaac was found.

God had instructed Abraham to get a wife for Isaac from his own people rather than from the local inhabitants.

In verses 4-7 Abraham SPEAKS aloud <u>what he had heard God say!</u> I want to add something right here. If you are not hearing God speak to you, it is because you are not listening, or you are tuned to the wrong station.

> 1 John 4:1 Beloved, believe not every spirit, but try the spirits whether
>
> they are of God: because many false prophets are gone out into the world.

Now here is a beautiful example of a man of God's choosing hearing God's instructions and following through.

> Genesis 24:4 But thou shalt go unto my country, and to my kindred, and take a wife unto my son Isaac.
>
> Genesis 24:5 And the servant said unto him, Peradventure the woman will not be willing to

follow me unto this land: must I needs bring thy son again unto the land from whence thou camest?

Genesis 24:6 And Abraham said unto him, Beware thou that thou bring not my son thither again.

Genesis 24:7 The LORD God of heaven, which took me from my father's house, and from the land of my kindred, and which spake unto me, and that sware unto me, saying, Unto thy seed will I give this land; he shall send his angel before thee, and thou shalt take a wife unto my son from thence.

Remember what Jesus said to His disciples?

John 12:49 "For I have not spoken of myself; but the Father which sent me, He gave me a commandment, what I should say, and what I should speak.

If Jesus in his earthly sojourn would speak only what He heard the Father speak, how much more should we speak only Gods words.

Now look at the prayer of the servant in verses 12-14.

Genesis 24:12 And he said, O LORD God of my master Abraham, I pray thee, send me good speed this day, and shew kindness unto my master Abraham.

> Genesis 24:13 Behold, I stand *here* by the well of water; and the daughters of the men of the city come out to draw water:

> Genesis 24:14 And let it come to pass, that the damsel to whom I shall say,

Let down thy pitcher, I pray thee, that I may drink; and she shall say, Drink, and I will give thy camels drink also: *let the same be* she *that* thou hast appointed for thy servant Isaac; and thereby shall I know that thou hast shewed kindness unto my master.

He believed the words of his master, Abraham, who believed the words of his master, God. Eliezer added words to assure that God, not he, would direct the whole operation. Then in verse 12 he looked in wonder as God's plan began to become clear to him. As he saw it unfold he did what we should do; verses 26 & 27, he worshipped God.

A personal note:

I remember as clearly as if this occurred yesterday, the evening when I walked to my favorite dreaming place with my dog "Blackie", and looked up to heaven and prayed this simple prayer. "Lord I ask for a wife who will love me just as I am."

When you are 14 years old and all the emotions of being a youth are raging within you, God understands and ministers to you in a way you can understand and if the desire is pure He will help you pray correctly.

This was a proper prayer. I did not know this until Nita and I had been married for over 40 years, but she, as a young girl prayed the very same prayer! Isn't God great?

Who put the prayer into the heart of Abraham, Eliezer, and Nita and me? A loving heavenly Father! For what purpose? to bring about His desire in the individual lives of His children.

I don't know if you have ever considered what we lost in the Garden of Eden when Adam sinned. But we lost the right of dominion over all of God's creation! <u>Before sin entered the world through disobedience, Adam and Eve spoke God's words and created much as God had.</u> They were instructed to tend and keep the garden or more properly all of what they were in charge of, had dominion over, which was actually all of God's creation!

God had given them control of the world, they gave it to God's adversary, and the rules changed. Consider this. If God had not given total dominion of His creation to mankind, man could not have given it away. If God had not given total dominion of His creation to mankind, and if man could not and did not give it away Paul would not have called Satan the god of this world! II Corinthians 4:4

God needs a man to speak and to do for Him in this world. This is why God instructs us to "Put me in remembrance: let us plead together: declare (say or speak) thou, that thou mayest be justified." Isaiah 43:26

Romans 2:17 gives us a key to God's instructions for creation. "and (God) calleth those things which are not as though they were."

In the "bara" creation which we studied in session one, we saw that original creation was accomplished by God, by first imagining what He wanted, then second speaking what He "saw" in His mind even though it was not visible to the human eye because it had not yet been manifested.

Three weeks is what it takes to change a habit or to create a new one. Do you want change in your life, the life of your spouse, and/or your marriage? Change your speech for the next three weeks.

Speak the end from the beginning.

Speak what you want to be.

Speak what you want your spouse to be.

Speak what you want your marriage to be.

In Mark 11:12-14 we see Jesus cursing a fig tree. This was done to teach a very important lesson to the disciples.

> Mark 11:12 And on the morrow, when they were come from Bethany, he was hungry:

> Mark 11:13 And seeing a fig tree afar off having leaves, he came, if haply he might find any thing thereon: and when he came to it, he found nothing but leaves; for the time of figs was not *yet*.

> Mark 11:14 And Jesus answered and said unto it, No man eat fruit of thee hereafter for ever. And his disciples heard *it*.

Look what happened when they passed that way again.

> Mark 11:20 And in the morning, as they passed by, they saw the fig tree dried up from the roots.
>
> Mark 11:21 And Peter calling to remembrance saith unto him, Master, behold, the fig tree which thou cursedst is withered away.
>
> Mark 11:22 And Jesus answering saith unto them, Have faith in God.
>
> Mark 11:23 For verily I say unto you, That whosoever shall say unto this mountain, Be thou removed, and be thou cast into the sea; and shall not doubt in his heart, but shall believe that those things which he saith shall come to pass; he shall have whatsoever he saith.
>
> Mark 11:24 Therefore I say unto you, What things soever ye desire, when ye pray, believe that ye receive *them,* and ye shall have *them.*
>
> Mark 11:25 And when ye stand praying, forgive, if ye have ought against any: that your Father also which is in heaven may forgive you your trespasses.
>
> Makr 11:26 But if ye do not forgive, neither will your Father which is in heaven forgive your trespasses.

We are to:

(1) have faith in God, not in ourselves or anyone or anything else.

(2) We are to speak to the mountains in our lives and cast them away.

(3) We are to forgive everyone for everything! Period! I hear people say; "I'll forgive but never forget." Bad decision, your sins will not be forgiven! Ouch.

(4) We are not to doubt in our heart that our words, which really are God's words, will accomplish what they were sent to do.

> Isaiah 55:11 "So shall the word be that goeth forth out of my mouth: it shall not return unto me void, but it shall accomplish that which I please, and it shall prosper in the thing whereto I sent it."

(5) We must believe that what we have spoken will be.

(6) We are to add to the spoken word our prayer asking for what we have spoken, continue to believe and then in an act of faith, receive that which we spoke into existence and asked for in prayer.

This seems too simple until we look at;

> James 4:3 "Ye ask, and receive not, because ye ask amiss, that ye may consume it upon your lusts."

We are to speak God's word over any desire we have or any request, that way we know we are not asking amiss. When we pray we are to pray in line with God's word and the end of all requests is to bring glory to God, not to use God's gifts to satisfy our lust.

A godly marriage is what God wants for us. We will have the joy in our relationship that only God can bring when we follow His plan. Marriage should be a joy inexpressible, full of the glory of God; a preview of heavenly joy and pleasure.

> The Jesus parallel in this lesson is, as Jesus created the world with images, words, and faith or belief in God's words, so let us create with and for our mate the marriage God intended us to have.
>
> We create the world in which we live with words we speak and believe.
>
> Our "Action for Creation" for this week is:
>
> I will speak good words of creation about my spouse and myself.

LOVE NOTES FROM JOHN
TO HIS LOVE

WHEN I LOOK AT YOUR FACE
I SEE NO ONE ELSE
AND NOTHING ELSE.
AND YOUR FACE IS ALWAYS
BEFORE ME.
YOU ARE MY
INSPIRATION.

Chapter 5

The Mystery of Marriage

Our "Action for Creation" for this week was:

I will speak good words of creation
about my spouse and myself.

So how are you doing? What changes are you beginning to see in each other, especially in yourselves? Our "Action for Creation" for this week was:

I will speak good words of creation about my spouse and myself

So how are you doing? What changes are you beginning to see in each other, especially in yourselves? Scripture readings for this week are:

Ephesians 5:28-33: The mystery of the parallel of Christ and the Church and man and wife, marriage.

> Genesis 1:27 & 2:24: God saw them as a single
> entity
> Genesis 3:22 God saw them sin as one entity.
> Genesis 3:17 Blame fell on Adam
> Genesis 3:17-24 Curse fell on both Adam and Eve
> as well as the earth.

The first 4 sessions were about the Majesty of marriage, beginning with the majesty of Man. This week we begin to look at the mystery of the marriage covenant. Let's look again at the instructions from Paul concerning the relationship of husbands and wives. Everything is as it should be, is understandable, proper and Christ-like. Then we come to verse 32. "This is a great mystery?" There is nothing mysterious about being a good husband or wife. What does he mean, mystery? In the next chapter we will look at the parallels between the marriage covenant and the New Covenant (Testament) Christ cut with us. Right now we must consider the mystery in order to understand the parallels and how important they are to the covenant.

> Ephesians 5:32 This is a great mystery: but I
> speak concerning Christ and the church.

> Ephesians 5:33 Nevertheless let every one of you
> in particular so love his wife even as himself; and
> the wife *see* that she reverence *her* husband.

What is this mystery that Paul was talking about? What is the correlation between the husband wife relationship and that of Jesus and the Church? I believe from the very beginning God has been telling us a truth about His plan for mankind and an even greater truth about Himself. If you were God, how would you reveal yourself to man? This was the dilemma, dilemma from our viewpoint, not God's. We have always had to have an example to see before we could understand God's plan. So, God gave us an example of His great love for us in the marriage covenant. We will consider this thought by taking another trip through the Bible starting in Genesis.

> Genesis 1:27 So God created man in his *own* image, in the image of God created he him; male and female created he them.

Take a look at Adam and Eve. They saw God each time they looked at each other, because they were created in God's image.

> Genesis 2:24 Therefore shall a man leave his father and his mother, and shall cleave unto his wife: and they shall be one flesh.

We see from the beginning, a man and woman were to leave everybody they were bound to, or related to, including their own parents, to establish this new entity. Then they were to hold unto this one other person until these two separate people became one new flesh. God sees them as <u>one</u> under His covenant of marriage. This was accomplished when they entered into a blood covenant, an unbreakable bond with each other, so that they could not be separated. In fact to break that bond would take the tearing of flesh, the cutting off of a part of a person, or in other words, death, and death had not entered into humanity and would not unless, or until, they sinned. In fact, they could not die or even know about death until they broke the covenant they had with God. Notice that everything written during this time, what is called "The Age of Innocence", has an everlasting connotation with no mention of an end of anything, just a continuation of life.

Then came that awful afternoon when everything changed.

> Genesis 3:17 And unto Adam he said, Because thou hast hearkened unto the voice of thy wife, and hast eaten of the tree, of which I commanded thee, saying, Thou shalt not eat of it: cursed *is* the ground for thy sake; in sorrow shalt thou eat *of* it all the days of thy life;

> Genesis 3:18 Thorns also and thistles shall it bring forth to thee; and thou shalt eat the herb of the field;

> Genesis 3:19 In the sweat of thy face shalt thou eat bread, till thou return unto the ground; for out of it wast thou taken: for dust thou *art,* and unto dust shalt thou return.

Notice in verse 17, the blame fell on Adam because he had been given charge over the Garden and had been told specifically not to do what he did, but in verses 18 and 19 we see the curse fell on all of creation.

> Gen 3:21 Unto Adam also and to his wife did the LORD God make coats of skins, and clothed them.

> Genesis 3:22 And the LORD God said, Behold, the man is become as one of us, to know good and evil: and now, lest he put forth his hand, and take also of the tree of life, and eat, and live for ever:

> Genesis 3:23 Therefore the LORD God sent him forth from the garden of Eden, to till the ground from whence he was taken.

> Genesis 3:24 So he drove out the man; and he placed at the east of the garden of Eden Cherubims, and a flaming sword which turned every way, to keep the way of the tree of life.

The result of sin is always death, God saw the sin as committed by both Adam and Eve, thus both paid the price as well as everything they had dominion over, all of creation.

This great mystery of the correlation between Christ and His Church and a man and his wife is beginning to come into view. You see, Adam, man, was charged with the sin of his wife because he did not confront it but rather became complicit with her by joining in the disobedience.

Jesus, the second Adam did not make the same mistake, but rather paid the price for mankind, took upon Himself the penalty of sin, that which should have been charged to mankind, thereby redeeming mankind and becoming our Savior. I have a question, what would have happened if Adam had done what Jesus did. If Adam had said to Eve, "Don't eat the forbidden fruit," and kept her from sinning? What if she had eaten it and Adam had said, "No, I will not partake, but instead I will intervene on your behalf with God and will pay the penalty required for your disobedience." What would God have done? Seeing what God did because of Jesus' sacrifice, I believe He would have accepted it and the curse would have been stopped.

We close this teaching with an outline of instructions for the husband and wife under the marriage covenant. Our next teaching will investigate these instructions in greater detail.

If we start at Ephesians 5:21, we see 4 commands for wives.

(1) Submit to husbands as to Christ. (v 22)
(2) Recognize headship of husbands. (v 23)
(3) Be subject to husbands. (v 24)
(4) Reverence husbands. (v 33)

There are 9 commands for husbands.

(1) Submit to one another including your wife (vs. 21)
(2) Be head of the wife. (v 23)
(3) Love wives as Christ loves the Church. (v 25)
(4) Love wives as own bodies. (v 28,33)

(5) Nourish, care for, protect, (v 29, 6:4; Rev. 12:6)

(6) Cherish; to foster, warm to ones bosom. (v 29; 1 Th. 2:7)

(7) Be joined as one flesh. (v 30-31)

(8) Leave parents for wives. (v 31)

(9) Cleave to wives. (v 31; Mt. 19:5)

Our first instruction shows that men are to love their wives as much as they love their own bodies! Then goes on to say that when a man loves his wife he is actually loving himself!!

The Jesus parallel in this lesson is the love I have for my wife should be as unconditional and devoted as the love Christ has for His Church. He cares for, nourishes and defends it both now and for eternity.

Our "Action for Creation" for this week is:

I will love and show my love to my spouse as Christ loves and shows His love to the Church.

LOVE NOTES FROM JOHN
TO HIS LOVE

You make my life a dance of joy!

Chapter 6

The Mystery of Marriage

Marriage as it parallels Christ and the Church

Our "Action for Creation" for this week was:

I will love and show my love to my spouse as
Christ loves and shows His love to the Church.

So how are you doing? What changes are you
beginning to see in each other, especially in yourselves?
Scripture readings for this week were:

> Ephesians chapter 5, plus look into the letters
> from Paul to the various Church's. Did you find
> other instructions concerning the responsibilities
> of the spouse to his/her mate?

The first 4 sessions were about the Majesty of
marriage. Last week we began to look at the mystery
of the marriage covenant. We continue today with

the parallels between the marriage covenant and the relationship or covenant between Christ and the Church. The purpose of the parallels is two fold. First we are able to see the reality of the great love God has for us, and second, we have a pattern to follow in developing and growing in our relationship with our spouses. When a question arises concerning our relationship, just look to Jesus. See what He has done and continues to do to show His unconditional love to you and me.

Let's start with the beginning of a relationship.

LOVE

> John 3:16 For God so loved the world, that he gave his only begotten Son, that whosoever believeth in him should not perish, but have everlasting life.

> John 17:23 I in them, and thou in me, that they may be made perfect in one; and that the world may know that thou hast sent me, and hast loved them, as thou hast loved

> John 17:24 Father, I will that they also, whom thou hast given me, be with me where I am; that they may behold my glory, which thou hast given me: for thou lovedst me before the foundation of the world.

How much does God love you? He loved you before there was a you! He loved you before He created the foundation of the world, let alone the earth and all its glory. Friend, there was no earth and He already had you in mind and loved you with an everlasting love, and He wrote your name down in the book of life, believing that when you came into the world you would answer His call to be His and He would take you into His family and give you the keys to His kingdom. Wow, He really loves you and me!

I know each of you have a story to tell, here is ours. Our story starts with a simple prayer when I was 14. "Lord send me a wife who will love me just as I am." I fell in love with Nita Raye then and there, I just hadn't met her yet and didn't know her name. When I was 25 I finally met her and I loved her before we had our first date, kissed or held hands. I had known her for only 5 weeks when I told my mother I'd met the woman I was to marry. We met on the Friday after Thanksgiving, 1965. On December 15th, or about 3 weeks later, I told Nita that I believed we could marry and never regret it. She said I was crazy.

You know, God is that way with us. He loved us before He laid the foundations of the world and made provisions for us to be with him.

COURTSHIP

Revelation 3:5 He that overcometh, the same shall be clothed in white raiment; and I will not blot out his name out of the book of life, but I will confess his name before my Father, and before his angels.

Once I knew Nita was the "one", I set about to court her, to pursue her, to be unbending in my pursuit. Jesus does the same for us. He lives in faith believing or acting like every human will accept him before they leave this earth as evidenced by his removal of their name from the Lamb's Book of life if they refuse him. There would be no reason to remove something if it wasn't there in the first place, written in faith and unconditional love. Then He tells everybody in Heaven from His Father to all the angels all about how wonderful you are and how much He loves you. Guess what, that is exactly what I did. I told everyone I talked to from my father and mother to anyone who would listen how wonderful Nita Raye was and I have a secret for you, one that will make your marriage beautiful beyond belief if you will do the same thing with your wife, or husband, I still do tell everyone who will listen how wonderful she is, 46 years later and counting.

PROPOSAL

> Matthew 11:28 Come unto me, all *ye* that labour and are heavy laden, and I will give you rest.

God is calling His man to come to Him and he never stops. He is pursuing the lost souls, pleading with them to "come home" as the old hymn says.

Not every man on bended knee proposes to his love. I assumed she wanted to be with me as much as I wanted to be with her. The weekend of Valentines Day

I said let's set a date, and we did. My father asked me if I thought I might be moving to quickly. I said if you have to think about it maybe you shouldn't do it. We exchanged our vows on April 14th, 1966, and we would do it all over again even knowing what all we would go through, because of our great love for each other. God knew from the foundation of the world what price would have to be paid by Him for our redemption and He still went ahead with our creation and then paid that horrific price because of His great love for us. Amazing!

The Lord Jesus will take any and every opportunity to whisk us into the family of God for those are His instructions from our Father.

THE CEREMONY

Acts 16:31 And they said, Believe on the Lord Jesus Christ, and thou shalt be saved, and thy house.

Romans 10:9 That if thou shalt confess with thy mouth the Lord Jesus, and shalt believe in thine heart that God hath raised him from the dead, thou shalt be saved.

God did all the hard work, all we have to do is believe and confess. Why do we have to confess that we believe in Him using words, and that we accept Jesus as Lord? Why can't we just believe in our hearts, sort of like a secret admirer might do? Because words are the tools God uses for creation and when you accept

Jesus as Lord and speak the words, you become a new creation.

> 2 Corinthians 5:17 Therefore if any man *be* in Christ, *he is* a new creature: old things are passed away; behold, all things are become new.

Think about the marriage vows for a moment.

I_____ take thee,_____ to be my wedded wife/husband to have and to hold, from this day forward, for better, for worse, for richer, for poorer, in sickness and in health, to love and to cherish, till death us do part, according to God's holy ordinance; and thereto I plight thee my troth."

When you are joined together in a marriage covenant you become "one flesh" or one with each other.

> Genesis 2:24 Therefore shall a man leave his father and his mother, and shall cleave unto his wife: and they shall be one flesh.

Again we see the parallel between Christ and the Church and a man and his wife.

Just as "til death do us part" is part of the marriage covenant, so Jesus said:

> Hebrews 13:5 *Let your* conversation *be* without covetousness; *and be* content with such things as ye have: for he hath said, I will never leave thee, nor forsake thee.

Never is a long time.

THE HONEYMOON

Acts chapters 2-4 detail the excitement of the new believers. We see a definite parallel between the attitude of these and a newly married couple. All things are possible! God has done great things and continues to do them. Each miracle only confirmed their faith.

The world is our oyster! That is what we felt when we began our life together. It can't get any better than this!

Jesus has promised us:

> 1 Peter 1:8 Whom having not seen, ye love; in whom, though now ye see *him* not, yet believing, ye rejoice with joy unspeakable and full of glory:

BUILDING A LIFE TOGETHER

> Galatians 2:1 Then fourteen years after I went up again to Jerusalem with Barnabas, and took Titus with *me* also.

Paul spent 14 years learning to know Jesus. Yes he taught Christians, he brought others to Christ, but these were the learning years, learning to know his Savior intimately.

In marriage we are to spend our time with each other. This is one of the reasons, perhaps the primary reason, we are to "forsake all others." Notice it did not say which gender. There is a Country Western song in which a lonely wife offers to turn their home into a bar just so her husband would spend evenings with her.

How sad. We are to forsake the single life to enjoy the new life with our love.

RULE 1: To have a blessed marriage we must spend time together developing a relationship so bound to each other that when we are apart, it hurts.

Look how David pleads with God after he sinned and repented. His all consuming desire was to have his relationship with God restored. Nothing was as important to him as that relationship.

Psalms 51:11-12: Cast me not away from thy presence; and take not thy Holy Spirit from me. Restore unto me the joy of thy salvation; and uphold me with thy free spirit."

BECOMING ONE

> John 17:23 I in them, and thou in me, that they may be made perfect in one; and that the world may know that thou hast sent me, and hast loved them, as thou hast loved me.

Nita Raye and I have reached that beautiful point of being so one with each other that we miss the closeness of that oneness when apart for even a moment. We are so "one" that we think, act and really are one. Christ in each of us has tied us together inseparable till death us do part.

> Ephesians 4:13 Till we all come in the unity of the faith, and of the knowledge of the Son of God, unto a perfect man, unto the measure of the stature of the fullness of Christ:

The Jesus parallel in this lesson is I am to live the parallels as God shows them to me so that I am always treating my spouse as Christ treats the Church.

Our "Action for Creation" for this week is:

When I look at my spouse I will remember I am looking at Christ who lives within him or her.

LOVE NOTES FROM JOHN
TO HIS LOVE

IF ALL THE WOMEN
IN THE WORLD
WERE IN THIS PLACE,
I WOULD STILL ONLY SEE
YOU

Chapter 7

The Mystery of Marriage

Treatment of husband and wife parallels Christ and the Church

Our "Action for Creation" for this week was:

When I look at my spouse I will remember I am looking at Christ who lives within him or her.

So how are you doing? What changes are you beginning to see in each other, especially in yourselves? Scripture readings for this week are:

Galatians 3:28: in Gods eyes we are equals;
Galatians 4:19: Christ is being formed in each of us. Galatians 5:13-15;19--23 by love serving one another
Colossians 3:12-14;18-19 mercy, kindness and long suffering

I Corinthians 7:3-5 power over our bodies belongs to the other.
Philippians 2:3&14 esteem each other better
Philippians 4:4-8 rejoice
Galatians 6:7 the law of sowing and reaping
I Corinthians 13:1-8 Love
I Corinthians 15:33 evil communications

That's a lot of Scriptures! But the responsibilities of the married person begin with understanding who we are in the eyes of God.

Galatians 3:28 There is neither Jew nor Greek, there is neither bond nor free, there is neither male nor female: for ye are all one in Christ Jesus.

If equals in God's eyes, then we must treat each other as equals. We are not to try to lord it over one another or try to "get one up" on each other. We are no better and no worse than our spouse in God's eyes. We must be the "God-like" species because we are the only one of God's creatures of whom Jesus prayed;

John 17:23 I in them, and thou in me, that they may be made perfect in one; and that the world may know that thou hast sent me, and hast loved them, as thou hast loved me.

Jesus did not pray this for cows or dogs or any other of his creation. He only prayed this for you and me, mankind, God-like creatures.

Galatians4:19 My little children, of whom I travail in birth again until Christ be formed in you,

Christ is being formed in each of us. What is the purpose of God creating Christ in us? This is a process. God is forming Christ in us until we join Him in Heaven. Upon entrance into God's heaven we will be perfect in all aspects, just like Jesus.

Galatians 5:13 For, brethren, ye have been called unto liberty; only *use* not liberty for an occasion to the flesh, but by love serve one another.

Galatians 5:19 Now the works of the flesh are manifest, which are *these;* Adultery, fornication, uncleanness, lasciviousness,

Galatians 5:20 Idolatry, witchcraft, hatred, variance, emulations, wrath, strife, seditions, heresies,

Galatians5:21 Envyings, murders, drunkenness, revellings, and such like: of the which I tell you before, as I have also told *you* in time past, that they which do such things shall not inherit the kingdom of God.

Galatians 5:22 But the fruit of the Spirit is love, joy, peace, longsuffering, gentleness, goodness, faith,

Galatians 5:23 Meekness, temperance: against such there is no law.

How do we reach this lofty goal? By serving one another in love. By acting just like Jesus who emulated his Father. Jesus came to serve, so must we, especially in our marriages.

> Colossians 3:12 Put on therefore, as the elect of God, holy and beloved, bowels of mercies, kindness, humbleness of mind, meekness, longsuffering;

> Colossians 3:13 Forbearing one another, and forgiving one another, if any man have a quarrel against any: even as Christ forgave you, so also *do* ye.

> Colossians 3:14 And above all these things *put on* charity, which is the bond of perfectness.

> Colossians 3:18 Wives, submit yourselves unto your own husbands, as it is fit in the Lord.

> Colossians3:19 Husbands, love *your* wives, and be not bitter against them.

> Colossians 3:20 Children, obey *your* parents in all things: for this is well pleasing unto the Lord.

Are we to show mercy, kindness and long suffering in all areas of life?

Yes!

Isn't it interesting how much easier it is to die for someone in a heroic way, than it is to live for them by serving them?

> I Corinthians 7:3 Let the husband render unto the wife due benevolence: and likewise also the wife unto the husband.

> I Corinthians 7:4 The wife hath not power of her own body, but the husband: and likewise also the husband hath not power of his own body, but the wife.

> I Corinthians 7:5 Defraud ye not one the other, except *it be* with consent for a time, that ye may give yourselves to fasting and prayer; and come together again, that Satan tempt you not for your incontinency.

Are you telling me that the power over our bodies belongs to my husband/wife? Even in areas of my space or my life.

Yes.

> Philippians 2:3 *Let* nothing *be done* through strife or vainglory; but in lowliness of mind let each esteem other better than themselves.

> Philippians 2:14 Do all things without murmurings and disputings:

How can I possibly do this? God's instructions are simple. Esteem the other person better than yourself. Obedience brings blessings, period! Just do it! And do it without complaining. Any time I find myself complaining, I say; "John Henry, (Henry is my middle name, don't laugh now), Just remember what God did to the Israelites when they complained! You don't have

40 years to wander in a desert or even in Omaha, Nebraska."

Another thing, when you are obedient, you'll be surprised by this, but you will rejoice. The Holy Spirit will fill your spirit with praises to God and they will literally spill out of your mouth and refresh you like springs of living water! Hallelujah again!!

> Philippians 4:4 Rejoice in the Lord alway: *and* again I say, Rejoice.
>
> Philippians 4:5 Let your moderation be known unto all men. The Lord *is* at hand.
>
> Philippians 4:6 Be careful for nothing; but in every thing by prayer and supplication with thanksgiving let your requests be made known unto God.
>
> Philippians 4:7 And the peace of God, which passeth all understanding, shall keep your hearts and minds through Christ Jesus.
>
> Philippians 4:8 Finally, brethren, whatsoever things are true, whatsoever things *are* honest, whatsoever things *are* just, whatsoever things *are* pure, whatsoever things *are* lovely, whatsoever things *are* of good report; if *there be* any virtue, and if *there be* any praise, think on these things.

And rejoice, always rejoice! Do it in sufferings, in abundance, in trials, in everything, rejoice, rejoice, rejoice and again I say rejoice! You are a child of Almighty God!!

Hallelujah! Oh, just get down and praise your Father for everything! Just do it!!

As in all thing of God there is a law. This one is the law of sowing and reaping.

> Galatians 6:7 Be not deceived; God is not mocked: for whatsoever a man soweth, that shall he also reap.

When we live this servant life we are sowing seeds of love and love must come back to us, many times over.

Let's talk about "Agape" love. The God kind of love. When God says he is love, do you think He means the Hollywood kind of love? Of course not. Look at what He says love is.

> 1Corinthians 13:1 Though I speak with the tongues of men and of angels, and have not charity, I am become *as* sounding brass, or a tinkling cymbal.

> 1Corinthians 13:2 And though I have *the gift of* prophecy, and understand all mysteries, and all knowledge; and though I have all faith, so that I could remove mountains, and have not charity, I am nothing.

> 1CoCorinthians 13:3 And though I bestow all my goods to feed *the poor,* and though I give my body to be burned, and have not charity, it profiteth me nothing.

1Corinthians 13:4 Charity suffereth long, *and* is kind; charity envieth not; charity vaunteth not itself, is not puffed up,

1Corinthians 13:5 Doth not behave itself unseemly, seeketh not her own, is not easily provoked, thinketh no evil;

1Corinthians13:6 Rejoiceth not in iniquity, but rejoiceth in the truth;

1Corinthians13:7 Beareth all things, believeth all things, hopeth all things, endureth all things.

1Corinthians13:8 Charity never faileth: but whether *there be* prophecies, they shall fail; whether *there be* tongues, they shall cease; whether *there be* knowledge, it shall vanish away.

When questions arise over how we are to act or react to a person, use these Scriptures as your guide. Just a quick word about evil communications.

I Corinthians 15:33 Be not deceived: evil communications corrupt good manners.

A word of caution. All that you do and say that is in line with God's word can be negated by you with words! Yes, the very tool we use to bless God and man, including yourself, if used incorrectly, can be used for evil.

The Jesus parallel in this lesson is: My responsibility is to Jesus Christ. Whatever I do to or for my spouse I am doing to and for Jesus.

Our "Action for Creation" for this week is:

I am to treat my wife/husband as if what
I do to them, I am doing to Jesus.

LOVE NOTES FROM JOHN
TO HIS LOVE

EVERY MORNING
BEGINS A FRESH
NEW SPARKLING WORLD
WITH YOU BY MY SIDE

Chapter 8

The Mystery of Marriage

Sexual Relations in a Christian Marriage

Our "Action for Creation" for this week was:

I am to treat my wife/husband as if what
I do to them I am doing to Jesus.

So how are you doing? What changes are you
beginning to see in each other, especially in yourselves?
Scripture readings for this week were:

Hebrews 13:4: marriage bed is undefiled
I Thessalonians 4:3-7: possess your own vessel,
(body) Song of Solomon: sing a song of love to
your spouse
Proverbs 5:15-19: be satisfied with your own
spouse
Proverbs 6:32: adultery destroys
I Corinthians 6:16 adultery makes another "one"
flesh!

God gave us, the "God-like" species, the gift of <u>sexual relations</u>. Other creatures use "sex" as a reproductive action exclusively. Only man has the gift of an experience that goes beyond reproduction, to calm us, to heal us, to provide relief from the stress of the day and give us a longer, more satisfying and gratifying life.

When I was 18 years old I worked in a dry cleaning plant in a city where my father pastured a Church. I mention that fact because my boss was aware of my beliefs and talked to me one day about the frustration he was experiencing in his marriage because his Priest believed that sexual activity was only for reproduction and all other sexual activity was sinful! That made for some very unhappy and unsatisfied people, and rightfully so. Sexual satisfaction is a gift from God, Enjoy your gift!

The marriage bed is undefiled

> Hebrews 13:4 Marriage *is* honorable in all, and the bed undefiled: but whoremongers and adulterers God will judge.

The first thing God wants us to know in reference to our Christian marriage bed experience is that there is a purity to it; that He has created it, blessed it and condones it. It is not defiled in any way. Pat Robertson in his book, 'The Secret Kingdom', answers a number of questions about sex. His comments on the marriage bed state his opinions, however he states that we should be led in this area as we are in others;

follow the Spirit's leading. This scripture says to us, that relations between husband and wife are pure. We can take from this that we are to enjoy each other sexually with joy and rejoicing just as we are to enjoy each other in other activities and in every other way.

We are not to act like unbelievers, involved in uncleanness, or sexual improprieties, but rather put our bodies under the control of the spirit.

> I Thessalonians 4:3-7: possess your own vessel, (body or spouse)
>
> I Thessalonians 4:3 For this is the will of God, *even* your sanctification, that ye should abstain from fornication:
>
> I Thessalonians 4:4 That every one of you should know how to possess his vessel in sanctification and honour;
>
> I Thessalonians 4:5 Not in the lust of concupiscence, even as the Gentiles which know not God:

This passage refers to one of two things.

(1) To a man's own body which he is to keep from fornication.
(2) To the wife whom the man is privileged to possess in a marriage relationship.

The primary responsibility always falls to the man. It is his duty to control himself and regardless of the temptation, he is to keep himself solely for his wife, as she does for him.

Song of Solomon:

Sing a song of love to your spouse. Read through the book, the concept is obvious. We have talked about it from lesson one. Just as we are to make a joyful noise unto the Lord, so are we to sing songs of love to our spouses.

Be satisfied with your own spouse.

> Proverbs 5:15 Drink waters out of thine own cistern, and running waters out of thine own well.

> Proverbs 5:16 Let thy fountains be dispersed abroad, *and* rivers of waters in the streets.

> Proverbs 5:17 Let them be only thine own, and not strangers' with thee.

> Proverbs 5:18 Let thy fountain be blessed: and rejoice with the wife of thy youth.

> Proverbs5:19 *Let her be as* the loving hind and pleasant roe; let her breasts satisfy thee at all times; and be thou ravished always with her love.

Our culture tends to glorify all sexual expression by and between any and all beings regardless of gender, age, or species. Just as we are instructed to be content with God's provision and commandments in other areas of our lives, so are we to be content with the spouse God chose for us.

You are to;

(1) Rejoice with your wife.
(2) Allow her breasts to satisfy you
(3) Be ravished with her love.

God is not bashful with his instructions to us about our sexual expressions. It is as if He has to say to us: "Hey! I made you to satisfy each other in this physical way. DO IT!!"

Adultery destroys

> Proverbs 6:32 *But* whoso committeth adultery with a woman lacketh understanding: he *that* doeth it destroyeth his own soul.

Just as Gods instructions are plain about our enjoyment of sex within the marriage covenant, so are His instructions about breaking that covenant. Here He states that this sin goes beyond a physical act, it actually destroys the soul.

Here are 6 results of adultery:

(1) Spiritual death: Proverbs vs.32; Romans 8:12-13.
(2) Physical death: Proverbs vs32; Lev. 20:10; Dt. 22:22
(3) Eternal death: Proverbs vs. 32; 1 Corinthians 6:9-10: Galatians 5:19-21: Revelation. 21:8;22:15.
(4) Dishonor
(5) Lasting reproach
(6) Blinding rage of husband.

Here another problem with adultery, it makes another "one" flesh!

> I Corinthians 6:16 What? know ye not that he which is joined to an harlot is one body? for two, saith he, shall be one flesh.

From this scripture we see that it is the physical act of sexual intercourse that causes two bodies to become "one flesh". But what if you are already married? How can you be one flesh with two? You can't, this and all other sexual deviation causes confusion. See Leviticus. 18:23

> Leviticus v 18:22 Thou shalt not lie with mankind, as with womankind: it *is* abomination.
>
> Leviticus 18:23 Neither shalt thou lie with any beast to defile thyself therewith: neither shall any woman stand before a beast to lie down thereto: it *is* confusion.
>
> Leviticus 18:24 Defile not ye yourselves in any of these things: for in all these the nations are defiled which I cast out before you:

Read verse 24 again, there is a national price to pay as well as a personal one. Billy Graham said one day that if God does not judge America for her sexual sins, He, God, would have to apologize to Sodom and Gomorra! Wow! Think about that then pray for our nation and pray for real revival.

Romans 1:26-28: & 29-32 results of confusion in sexual relations.

Romans 1:26 For this cause God gave them up unto vile affections: for even their women did change the natural use into that which is against nature:

Romans 1:27 And likewise also the men, leaving the natural use of the woman, burned in their lust one toward another; men with men working that which is unseemly, and receiving in themselves that recompence of their error which was meet.

Romans 1:28 And even as they did not like to retain God in *their* knowledge, God gave them over to a reprobate mind, to do those things which are not convenient;

Romans 1:29 Being filled with all unrighteousness, fornication, wickedness, covetousness, maliciousness; full of envy, murder, debate, deceit, malignity; whisperers,

Romans 1:30 Backbiters, haters of God, despiteful, proud, boasters, inventors of evil things, disobedient to parents,

Romans 1:31 Without understanding, covenantbreakers, without natural affection, implacable, unmerciful:

Romans 1:32 Who knowing the judgment of God, that they which commit such things are worthy of death, not only do the same, but have pleasure in them that do them.

RE: pornography

I can add nothing to the text except to say that we are living in a time of these very conditions. Why is pornography so horrendous? It corrupts the mind and imagination. The very gift God gave to man to enable him to co-create with Him, is being perverted to destroy man from the outside in. Man was made a spiritual being just like God. The spirit of man was to rule the soul, (mind), and the body. Sin caused an inversion. The body rules the man taken with pornography through the images in his mind, and the spirit who is supposed to rule, is abandoned.

The Jesus parallel in this lesson is: Our gift of intimate pleasure is to be enjoyed physically, mentally, and spiritually. It is an earthly mirror of the spiritual intimacy one can have with Jesus by spending time alone, quietly contemplating His glorious beauty.

Our "Action for Creation" for this week is:

Relish the gift of intimacy.

LOVE NOTES FROM JOHN
TO HIS LOVE

You are the rest of me

Chapter 9

The Mission of Marriage

Our "Action for Creation" for this week was:

Relish the gift of intimacy.

So how are you doing? What changes are you beginning to see in each other, especially in yourselves?

What is the responsibility of the husband to his wife? What is the responsibility of the wife to her husband?

In the previous 8 chapters we have looked at the majesty of marriage and the mystery of marriage, from here to the end of this teaching we will look at the mission of marriage. In the secular world the process looks something like this. Man meets woman, or boy meets girl, they feel a connection, which is really that the hormones are expressing themselves and all the books, movies, as well as their friends say that it is time to "hook up" or find out if you really belong together by having a sexual encounter. It's normal, it's natural, just do it and think about it later!

I think you can see the parallel here to what happened in the garden of Eden. Man was made a spirit being as the controlling force, the part that directed the soul, (mind, emotions, or the nesehe), to think, plan and do the bidding of the spirit which was doing the bidding of God the Father.

The physical part of man was to do three things. First it was to take directions from the mind as to accomplishing duties or tasks. Think about this a minute. The mind can not sow seeds, or harvest a crop, or hold hands with another person. It, the mind, can think about doing those things but it can not do them. A physical body must do what the mind has thought of and instructed it to do.

The second thing the body can do is gather information for the mind to process, and it does this through it's five physical senses, sight, hearing, feeling or touching, tasting and smelling. The mind takes the information gathered and very much like a computer gives directions. Here is an example. You see a beautiful flower on the other side of a fence and you climb the fence to pick it. What has happened? A physical sense, sight, desired a physical thing and set about to obtain it. Then something unexpected happened. The eyes see a bull running toward you because you entered his space! Your mind says, "Jump the fence to save your life!" And your body obeys your mind. Have you ever heard a noise so eerie that the hair on the back of your neck stood at attention? Your mind was saying run for your life there is something not right here!

The third thing the body can do is rebel, and that is what happened in the garden of Eden. To prove this look again at Genesis 3:6.

> Genesis 3:6 And when the woman saw that the tree *was* good for food, and that it *was* pleasant to the eyes, and a tree to be desired to make *one* wise, she took of the fruit thereof, and did eat, and gave also unto her husband with her; and he did eat.

The physical sense of sight added to the mental questioning of God's words and sin, or missing the mark, which is what sin means, occurred. What also occurred was an inversion of the triune man. Before the fall, man looked like this:

Spirit. The controller who received instructions from God the creator. Soul/mind: heard from the spirit and sent instructions to the body.

Body. The servant of the spirit and soul/mind carried out the instructions and everything worked perfectly in an orderly manner.

After sin entered the human spirit, through disobedience, the order of predominance was inverted so that the triune man looked like this:

Body. The lusts and desires of the physical became the driving force, demanding the soul/mind to justify it's actions, and quiet the longings of the spirit.

Soul/mind: It became subservient to the passions of the body.

Spirit: It became unable to act in defense of God's creation because the speech (physical sense, sound), of the body was in defiance of God but was in alliance with His enemy, the Devil, and now the Devil was able to rule the whole man by putting the body and it's desires in the commanding place.

You say, John is this a new teaching? No! Read this:

Genesis 6:5 And GOD saw that the wickedness of man *was* great in the earth, and *that* every imagination of the thoughts of his heart *was* only evil continually.

There was a real reason for Jesus to come into the world. It was to put things back in order, to allow His spirit to infuse the new creation, and now the new creation with the Spirit of God directing it is again the controlling force, instructing the renewed mind, the mind of Christ, to direct the body to do God's will again! Hallelujah!!

So, what does that mean to us in everyday situations? The real mission of marriage is to reveal to the world the love of God by being devoted to each other, loving each other or as I like to say, "Be Jesus to someone today. You may be the only Jesus they will ever see."

Now let us look at some of the ways we can demonstrate the love of God to those around us by our actions.

DUTIES OF A GODLY MAN

Genesis 3:23: Till the soil. (Work to provide for his family.
I Timothy 5:8: Man who does not provide has denied the faith.
Titus 2:6: Be sober minded.
Ephesians 5:25-33: Love wives as self.
Colossians 3:19: Love your wife and don't be bitter toward her.
I Peter 3:7: Husband to give honor to his wife so their prayers are not hindered.

DUTIES OF A GODLY WIFE

Genesis 4:1: Only the wife is given the privilege of bringing new life into the world.
Proverbs 31:10-31: The model wife.
Titus 2:4-5: She must be willing to learn and willing to teach.
Colossians 3:18 & Ephesians 5:22-24: Wife is to submit to husband as the Church is to submit to Christ.

DUTIES OF BOTH HUSBAND AND WIFE

Genesis 1:28: Be fruitful, multiply, subdue the earth and have dominion.
Genesis 2:15: Dress the garden and keep it.
Ecclesiastes 4:9-10: Two, husband and wife, are better than one.
Ephesians 5:19-21: Give God thanks and submit to each other.
I Peter 5:5-9: Submit AND humble yourselves to each other.

Philippians 2:5-8: Have the mind of Christ, humble yet equal.
Colossians 3:12-14: Forgive one another and forbear one another.

Man was not created to lay about doing nothing. Animals, birds, and fish were created to eat, sleep, and exercise, if you will. But man was given duties from the beginning.

Genesis 3:23: Till the soil----.

One of the problems the early church had is a problem in some Church's today. New believers can get the idea that as believers God will now supply all their needs without any effort on their part. The word says, not so. We are to provide first for our own families then for the family of believers and other needy folk.

Titus 2:6: Be sober minded.

Being sober minded means that we are to be wise. There was a culture of indulgence and debauchery that permeated the lands Paul and the new church inhabited. Paul was advising Titus to not get involved in that, and to be sober about life. We have seen recently the failing of a 21st century pastor because he would not remain sober.

Ephesians 5:25-33: Love wives as self.

We have looked at this scripture before, but it is a requirement for the husbands. If we consider everything we do with this in mind we will obey the scriptures and delight our wives.

> *Colossians 3:19: Love your wife and don't be bitter toward her.*

This is an interesting scripture. Don't be bitter? All scripture travels parallel paths. If you love your wife as yourself you will not be bitter toward her.

> *I Peter 3:7: Husband to give honor to his wife so their prayers are not hindered.*

If your prayers are not being answered, don't blame God. Ask yourself; am I giving honor to my wife? This is such an explosive verse. Have you ever thought that God is so insistent about men honoring their wives that He refuses to answer your prayers unless you do?

DUTIES OF A GODLY WIFE

> *Genesis 4:1: Only the wife is given the privilege of bringing new life into the world.*

God has so greatly honored the female of the "god-like species", allowing only her to bring new beings into the world. What a privilege!

> *Proverbs 31:10-31: The model wife*

For all the women who have said that Christianity places women in a second-class status, I say "read the Word of God!" Look at what this woman does and how highly honored she is. She has her own business, spends her own money, cares for her family and her servants and her children, husband, and those who know her call her blessed

> *Titus 2:4-5: She must be willing to learn and willing to teach.*

To be a good teacher one must first be a good student. God instructs us to learn from the older people in the faith and then to pass on that wisdom. Also notice that women are teaching women.

> *Colossians 3:18 & Ephesians 5:22-24: Wife is to submit to husband as the Church is to submit to Christ.*

Submission is so misunderstood. Christ did not consider himself to be less than God when He submitted. He considered Himself to be equal with God, yet He submitted. Because of that submission, which accomplished God's will for mankind, God gave Jesus a name which is above every name in Heaven on earth and under the earth, that at His name every knee shall bow. One might call this the blessing of submission.

DUTIES OF BOTH HUSBAND AND WIFE

> *Genesis 1:28: Be fruitful, multiply, subdue the earth and have dominion.*

Husbands and wives are to be involved with the duties of being fruitful and keeping the earth under God's control as His regents. We are to have the dominance of the earth as the only "god-like species".

> *Genesis 2:15: Dress the garden and keep it.*

It appears Adam and Eve did tend the Garden of Eden, but they failed to keep it. They were instructed to keep intruders out. We as God's regents are to keep our "garden". God has planted us in a place to show His love and we are to protect that place.

> *Ecclesiastes 4:9-10: Two, husband and wife, are better than one.*

The scriptures in another place say "one will put a thousand to flight, but two will put ten thousand to flight. God has made us to need each other. Everything works better when we work together.

> *Ephesians 5:19-21: Give God thanks and submit to each other.*

Submitting to each other while grumbling about it doesn't work. We are to give thanks to God for the privilege of submission.

I Peter 5:5-9: Submit AND humble yourselves to each other.

Then God adds to the submission principle, humility. Be humble, do not exalt yourself. You have no reason to exalt yourself. The next breath you take is at the pleasure of God.

Philippians 2:5-8: Have the mind of Christ, humble yet equal.

The only way we can have the mind of Christ is to be humble.

The only way to be humble is to have the mind of Christ.

Colossians 3:12-14: Forgive one another and forbear one another.

To say "I forgive but I'll never forget" is not the Christian way to live. If you ever desire to hold a grudge, think of what God could hold against you! Forgive, forbear and live.

The Jesus parallel in this lesson is: Our responsibility in marriage is to emulate Christ.

Our "Action for Creation" for this week is:

I will submit and humble myself to my spouse.

LOVE NOTES FROM JOHN
TO HIS LOVE

WHEN I SEE YOU
I SEE ALL THE BEAUTY
AND LOVE OF GOD BUNDLED
IN ONE PERSON WHO
HE SO GREATLY LOVES
AND I REALIZE HOW MUCH
HE LOVES ME TO
GRANT ME YOU!

Chapter 10

The Mission of Marriage

Our children are to be loved and trained in the same manner as God loves and trains us. We are to exhibit a God like character thereby teaching our children by example how to live. We are the "living word of God" to our children...

Our "Action for Creation" for this week was:

I will submit and humble myself to my spouse.

So how are you doing? What changes are you beginning to see in each other, especially in yourselves? Scripture readings for this week were:

Deuteronomy 6:6&7: Duties of a parent.
Proverbs 22: 6: Train up a child.
Proverbs 13:24 Spare the rod, spoil the child.
Proverbs 3:11: Despise not the chastening of the Lord. Ephesians 6:4: Rear in the fear and

admonition of the Lord. Colossians 3:21: Provoke
not the children lest they become discouraged.
Deuteronomy 6:6&7: Duties of a parent.

As Moses is giving instructions to the people prior
to his departure he inserts this admonition.

"Teach the law of God diligently to your children."

Speak God's words and commandments while you
are in your home, when outside the home, at bedtime
and when you arise. The idea is to never stop speaking
God's words to them.

> Joshua 1:8 This book of the law shall not depart
> out of thy mouth; but thou shalt meditate therein
> day and night, that thou mayest observe to do
> according to all that is written therein: for then
> thou shalt make thy way prosperous, and then
> thou shalt have good success.

> Proverbs 22:6 Train up a child in the way he
> should go: and when he is old, he will not depart
> from it.

There is hope! Sometimes in our child rearing years
we think everything we say to the children goes in one
ear and out the other. Not so! It may take awhile but
in time the Godly teachings of a Godly parent will
take root and even the wayward child will come back
to God.

> Proverbs:13:24 He that spareth his rod hateth
> his son: but he that loveth him chasteneth him
> betimes.

Let's also look at:

> Proverbs: 19:18 Chasten thy son while there is
> hope, and let not thy soul spare for his crying.

Although there are a multitude of scriptures that deal with correction and punishment of children these two tell all that needs to be said. Children by nature will push authority to the limit just to find the boundaries. We as God's regents are to set the boundaries as God directs and as culture requires. These scriptures in no way condone beating a child nor mistreating a child, but they do demand that the parent correct the child and when necessary a swat on the behind is a proper result of improper behavior.

> Proverbs 3:11 My son, despise not the chastening
> of the LORD; neither be weary of his correction:

Whether we are receiving the correction, or we are meting it out, it is never pleasant. But punishment has a purpose, and that is to change direction. We are instructed not to despise God's chastisement or correction because it is positive proof that God LOVES us! The last spanking I gave to one of our children went like this. First, I explained why I was going to spank him. I explained that his behavior was unacceptable and would not be tolerated. Then I spanked him, not too hard, of course, then I hugged him and told him I loved him. Have you ever noticed that God does it the same way?

> Ephesians 6:4 And, ye fathers, provoke not your children to wrath: but bring them up in the nurture and admonition of the Lord.

Notice this instruction is given to the fathers. Two dynamics come into play here. First there is the ever present desire of the father to hold back the son from taking his eventual place as the heir of the family until the son is ready, which normally does not happen until the death or disabling of the father. Second is the natural drive of the son to supplant his father. We see the results of incorrect father son relations in the Priest Eli and his two disobedient sons whose distain for God's directions and Eli's refusal to correct them cost them their lives. And we all know of the horrific results of King David's neglect of his sons. His oldest tried to overthrow David and kill him; the next in line killed the third in line for raping their sister. Only Solomon was found fit in God's eyes to inherit the Kingdom, yet his lack of proper instruction from his father David caused him to make many errors in judgment.

> Colossians 3:21 Fathers, provoke not your children *to anger,* lest they be discouraged.

In Ephesians we are instructed not to provoke our children to wrath or anger, here we are told why. Just as our words to and about our spouse are always to be building up words, our words and actions toward our children are to be encouraging and building up words.

Just as God encourages us, we are to encourage our children.

Just as God loves us, we are to love our children.

Just as God forgives us, we are to forgive our children.

We are to be kind and loving and gentle and forgiving so that when we teach our children to call God, Father, the image that comes to their mind is one of unconditional love.

The Jesus parallel in this lesson is: We are to train our children in the ways of the Lord by teaching them what the Lord has taught us.

Our "Action for Creation" for this week is:

We will love and train our children as God does us.

LOVE NOTES FROM JOHN
TO HIS LOVE

You taught me how to be a good father by being
a wonderful loving mother to our children

Chapter 11

The Mission of Marriage

*The marriage is to be a reflection of God's love
to all God's creation but especially to mankind.*

Our "Action for Creation" for this week was:

We will love and train our children as God does us.

So how are you doing? What changes are you beginning to see in each other, especially in yourselves? Scripture readings for this week were:

Ephesians 5:1-2: Be followers of Christ, reflect Him.
Galatians 4:19: Until Christ be formed in you.
John 17:21-23: That we may be one with Christ.
Ephesians 5:1-2: Be followers of Christ, reflect Him.

How difficult it would be to live a good and godly life without an example to follow. We are instructed to live as children following the pattern of our Father

God's love toward us. We are to walk in love. What does that mean? We are to follow Jesus' example. We are to give ourselves completely to the other without concern for ourselves or our needs. Follow Jesus. He gave himself as an offering and a sacrifice to God to benefit mankind. When we give ourselves to each other selflessly we are giving ourselves to God as an offering and sacrifice which is a delight to Him.

Galatians 4:19: Until Christ be formed in you.

Paul was telling the Galatians that through prayer he, Paul, Was "birthing them again until Christ be formed in you." This passage gives us an astounding truth. Jesus Christ is to be formed in each of us! He, Christ, is to live in and through us each day, every day, always. "For it is no longer I who live but Christ in me-." One of the great mysteries of the Christian marriage is that Christ lives within each of us so when I love my wife or when she loves me we are loving Christ. The world can now see Jesus Christ by seeing the love of this married couple. The spirit of those looking at us see through the exterior and see love; (for God is love.) and they are drawn to that love, giving us an opportunity to share the source of our love with them. This is one way the Father draws the world to Himself.

If the world sees a Christian couple fighting or hating each other, how can they see Christ? They can't. They think believers are no different than anyone else.

Why? When we act like the world, the love of God cannot shine through.

John 17:21-23: That we may be one with Christ.

Can you see the progression of truth coming out? First in Ephesians we read that we are to be followers of Christ. In Galatians we see Christ is to be formed in us. Now we go the most important prayer ever prayed. If anyone's prayers are heard and answered, Jesus' are! Jesus prayed that you and I would be one with Him and the Father. Let's look at this from the marriage standpoint.

Jesus asked the Father to do the following;

> Make the husband and wife one just as Jesus and his Father are one;
>
> Make the husband and wife one IN the Father and Jesus!
>
> To what end? That the world may believe that the Father sent Jesus into the world.
>
> Why and how? by seeing the essence, (love), of God in the love shown between the husband and wife. The great mystery is revealed. See a loving Christian couple; see God revealed in human flesh again, for God is love.

When we give this demonstration to the world, God gives us a gift; the glory which God gave to Jesus is given to us! It is this glory that gives us the ability to be one with each other in the same way that Jesus and God are one.

The conclusion is this.

> God is in Jesus; Jesus is in us; we are in each other and together we are ONE.

The purpose is to show the world that God the Father sent Jesus into the world to let them know He loves all of us as much as He loves Jesus, His only begotten Son.

The Jesus parallel in this lesson is: as Jesus reflected the Fathers love to mankind, we are to reflect Christ's love to our husbands and wives.

Our "Action for Creation" for this week is:

I will be a mirror of Jesus' love to my spouse.

LOVE NOTES FROM JOHN
TO HIS LOVE

If there had never been a you or me on this earth, my love for you is so strong that the stars of heaven could have heard from the farthest reaches of the universe, my voice calling, "Nita Raye, Nita Raye"

Chapter 12

The Mission of Marriage REVEALED

Review and challenge

Our "Action for Creation" for this week was:

I will be a mirror of Jesus' love to my spouse.

So how are you doing? What changes are you beginning to see in each other, especially in yourselves? Scripture readings for this week were:

John 17:21-23: That we may be one with Christ. Ephesians 5:28-33: The mystery of the parallel of Christ and the Church and man and wife, marriage.

Our lessons are at an end. Yet in reality they have just begun, because we now have a fuller understanding of who we are, and what we are to do to enjoy a "God" kind of relationship in our marriages.

We asked the question at the beginning; "What is the mystery Paul was talking about in Ephesians?" we now have the answer!

Jesus spoke plainly and definitively in His prayer recited in John 17:21-23. Let's begin at the conception of this truth.

In the beginning God created mankind in His own likeness, we know that, but have we considered that man had:

God's mind?

God's thoughts?

God's goals?

God's plans?

God's interests at heart?

In fact, we could say in God's eyes, man was created just a little lower than Himself, has all of His, (God's) attributes, and only on His throne does God consider Man to be under Him.

Man and woman were really one with God in every aspect of their lives.

SIN CHANGED ALL THAT ONE AFTERNOON!

JESUS REVERSED THE CURSE ON A
CROSS ON ANOTHER AFTERNOON!

Our covenant through Jesus gives us all the benefits of the first covenant plus all the benefits Jesus has with the Father!

We are ONE with God and ONE with Jesus and ONE with each other!

When I look at Nita, I see Jesus! Because He lives in her. When she smiles at me, I see Jesus. When she holds my hand, I am holding Jesus' hand. When we laugh we are laughing with Jesus. This oneness is what Jesus came to restore. I am now one with God, one with Jesus, and one with Nita, what a wonderful way to live in joy.

The challenge we must now face is to live out our knowledge and convictions. We have the option of forgetting all we have learned and do the things we have always done and watch nothing change.

Or we can decide to repent, change directions and "prove" God's word by loving, living for and revering our mates, the person God chose for us to love, and watch as God changes both of us to be like Him, pure love, unconditional, unending, sacrificing all that I am for _____(Nita.)

The Jesus parallel in this teaching is: as Jesus reflected the Fathers love to mankind, so are we to reflect His love to the world through the marriage covenant.

Our "Action for Creation" for the rest of our lives:

> I will treat my spouse as I would Jesus because
> we are one with Him.

And continue to:

(1) Compliment your mate, refuse to criticize.
(2) Speak only building up words to and about your spouse.
(3) It is no longer I who live but we, for we are one.
(4) I will speak good words of creation about my spouse and myself.
(5) I will love and show my love to my spouse as Christ loves and shows His love to the Church.
(6) When I look at my spouse, I will remember I am looking at Christ who lives within him or her.
(7) I am to treat my wife/husband as if what I do to them I am doing to Jesus.
(8) I will relish God's gift of intimacy.
(9) I will submit and humble myself to my spouse.
(10) We will love and train our children as God does us.
(11) I will be a mirror of Jesus' love to my spouse.
(12) I will treat my spouse as I would Jesus because we are one with Him.

May God richly bless your marriage as you live in obedience to His plan.

Postscript

Why are we called Christians? And why is that important? If you have read the book of Ruth, you know the answer in an allegory.

Ruth, the daughter in law of Naomi, came back to Bethlehem with Naomi after both of their husband died while living in Moab, during a famine in Israel. When she walked down the street, the local women commented on what a wonderful thing she had done for her mother in law to care for Naomi in her old age, BUT, nevertheless, she was a Moabite, a hated people by the Jews and therefore not of God's chosen people.

Then Boaz a man of great wealth an importance married her, and the ladies no longer called her, Ruth the Moabite, she was now Ruth the wife of Boaz, a highly respected member of their society!

What happened? She was still Ruth, but a covenant had been cut, or entered into, between Ruth and Boaz and that covenant gave her a new name and a new identity.

When a woman marries a man, she takes his last name, (usually and customarily), as her own. Notice something, I believe is very important. She does not give up her first or middle name, because she is still an individual with her own ambitions, needs and desires. Only her last name was changed. But Nita Raye by taking my last name came under my protection and all that I would inherit or accumulate in our lifetime was as much hers as it was mine and she became through our marriage covenant, a blood member of my family past, present and future.

When you were born you entered the world as a human being or Adam, created a "God like being." When you accepted Jesus Christ as your redeemer, He gave you His last name to signify what family you now belonged to.

I am John Henry Dumke Christian! Hallelujah!

LOVE NOTES FROM JOHN
TO HIS LOVE

When I touch you, I touch the edge of the curtain that separates time from eternity, and I know what Heaven feels like.